DIVINE ASCENT

PETER O. OLATUNBOSUN

COPYRIGHT PAGE

Title of the Book: DIVINE ASCENT: EMBRACING YOUR ROLE AS A CANDIDATE FOR PROGRESS

Author: PETER O. OLATUNBOSUN

Copyright © [2024]

ISBN 978 – 97 – 8 – 769794 - 8

Request for information on this title should be addressed to
The Publisher:
petfav001@gmail.com
Abundance Media Incorporation

PREFACE

The word of God says all good and perfect gifts come from God. Our heavenly father delights in blessing his children with an enviable life because He wants to show us off to the world. He does this by supporting us to live a meaningful life and by empowering us to live lives that glorify His name.

The Holy Spirit prompted me to write this book. He instructed me to draw from the cisterns of life to quench the thirst of the people of God. The necessity of water for the survival of man is symbolic of the revelation of God's word to the child of God. His breakthrough, dominion, peace, and fulfillment all rest on the authority the word of God has over his life.

This book will show you how to scripturally fulfill your destiny. As you feed your spirit with instructions from God's word through the pages of this book, I see you living the victorious life that God planned for you.

God can meet every need. He has never failed, and He will not start failing with you. He is not interested in making you a Guinea pig! The scriptures, on several occasions, indicate that there is nothing impossible with God.

As you are precious in His sight, your case is neither cold nor closed. Your destiny will find fulfillment!

I urge you to read this book with an open heart. Prophet Isaiah says in his book, Isaiah 29:11–12:

> "[11] And the vision of all is become unto you as
> the words of a book that is sealed, which men
> deliver to one that is learned, saying, Read this, I
> pray thee: and he saith, I cannot; for it is sealed:

^{12} And the book is delivered to him that is not
learned, saying, Read this, I pray thee: and he
saith, I am not learned"

Isaiah 29: 11-12

Satanic limitations will give way to the revelation of the
word of God. The understanding and application of the word
of God usher a revolution into the life of the child of God.
As you digest the contents of this Holy Spirit-inspired book,
expect the miraculous to happen because it is bound to, as
written in 1 Corinthians 2:9–10.

"^{9}But as it is written, Eye hath not seen, nor ear
heard, neither have entered into the heart of
man, the things which God hath prepared for
them that love him. ^{10}But God hath revealed
them unto us by his Spirit: for the Spirit
searcheth all things, yea, the deep things of God.

I welcome you to a new life of supernatural discoveries!

You shall no longer be stranded in the journey of life in the
mighty name of Jesus!

In His service,

Peter Olatunbosun

DEDICATION

To the Holy Spirit, the true Author of progress and inspiration. This work is a testament to Your guidance and grace.

TABLE OF CONTENT

CHAPTER 1

CHOSEN FOUNDATIONS

For other foundation can no man lay than that is laid, which is Jesus Christ.

In order to begin your path as a candidate for advancement, you must first get an awareness of your foundation which is in Christ Jesus. The bedrock of your life is its foundation, which in turn establishes its tone. Your ethics and beliefs are some of the elements that form your foundation.
Jesus Christ expects us to build our lives on His teachings (1 Corinthians 3:11). By so doing, we can focus on the truly important things. The stronger our foundation is, the easier it will be for us to make progress in our lives. A compromised foundation truncates the growth of well-meaning Christians.

Chosen Foundations is the groundwork for your ascent to a life of divine progress.

The Divine Blueprint: Unveiling Your Purpose
Much like an artist's intentional strokes on his canvas, your creator's brush designed your destiny deliberately and purposefully. There were no loose ends, and nothing escaped His attention. We will unveil the clear and defined pathways to your already-designed destiny. Your purpose, intricately woven into your being, is the compass guiding you on the journey of progress. This is the time to unravel this mystery and discover the reason for your existence.

This was established long before you made your entry into this world.

> "⁵Before I formed you in the womb I knew you,
> before you were born I set you apart; I appointed
> you as a prophet to the nations.

> Jeremiah 1:5

Unveiling your divine blueprint is not an intellectual exercise. It is a journey of self-discovery. Using the divine blueprint, you have a clear and defined pathway for your life. This will, in no small measure, help you align with God's predetermined design for your life.

From Genesis to Revelation: Tracing the Path of Progress

Humans are wired for progress, and they habitually seek to chart a course for it. We must understand our purpose pathway to be able to key into it. We are invited on a voyage through the scriptures, where progressive narratives of people appear time and time again. Their stories will inspire us to chart our own course, guiding us on the path of divine progress.

We meet iconic individuals who, despite their flaws and imperfections, embraced their roles as candidates for progress. Abraham, the father of faith, dared to embark on a journey without knowing the destination. Moses, a reluctant leader, guided the Israelites out of Egypt through the wilderness on a turbulent journey. David, the shepherd boy turned king, danced before the Ark of the Covenant, selflessly worshiping God, not minding who was watching.

Their stories tug at our heartstrings, beckoning us to find our place in God's grand scheme of things. In the tales of triumphs and tribulations, victories and defeats, lies the inspiration to press on, knowing that your story is an integral part of the whole picture. These testimonies should breathe new life into your journey, stirring a sense of purpose like never before.

Faith: Your Firm Foundation

Faith is the cornerstone of progress; is trust and belief in someone or something. By doing so, you are propelled to take actions you otherwise may not have taken. Without it, your resolve to fulfill purpose will not be firm. You must accompany it with works to make it effective.

> "[26]As the body without the spirit is dead, so faith without deeds is dead.

> James 2:26

Consider the patriarchs of old, who, by faith, navigated unknown territories, built arks in anticipation of floods, and conquered kingdoms against overwhelming odds. You must be an active participant in the divine construction project of your life. Each step taken in faith lays another brick, solidifying the structure of progress.

Your role in God's master plan is not immaterial. It is a pivotal part of your redemption and restoration. Your faith, when activated, becomes a catalyst for divine intervention. It transforms obstacles into opportunities and setbacks into comebacks. You are a progressive person, charting your course through life, holding on tenaciously to faith.

Sacred Skills: Equipping Yourself for Divine Progress

Progress does not occur in the absence of other variables. It will not happen out of the blue. Progress requires the intentional cultivation of talents, skills, attributes, and attitudes. When you throw education - formal or informal, and lifelong learning into the mix, you set yourself up for a life that shines brighter as the days go by.

> "[18]The path of the righteous is like the morning sun, shining ever brighter till the full light of days
>
> Proverbs 4:18

Equipping yourself for divine progress means that you are taking practical steps to apprehend your purpose. Let's take a look at some of the skills required to make progress.

Progress is never a spontaneous event, nor does it occur in isolation. It demands the deliberate nurturing of talents, skills, attributes, and attitudes. True progress unfolds when you actively cultivate these qualities with intention. And when you add education—whether formal or informal—and embrace lifelong learning, you ignite a transformative process. This dynamic fusion not only propels you forward but sets the stage for a life that grows richer and more radiant with each passing day. It's the spark that turns potential into brilliance, ensuring your path is ever-illuminated.

5 keys to making progress

Here are five essential keys to making progress:

1. Clear Vision and Goals: Progress begins with knowing where you're headed. Setting specific,

measurable, and realistic goals gives you direction and purpose. A clear vision acts as your roadmap, guiding you through challenges and ensuring you stay focused.

2. Consistent Action: Success is built on the foundation of consistent effort. Small, steady steps forward accumulate over time. Prioritize action over perfection, and develop daily habits that push you closer to your objectives.

3. Adaptability and Resilience: Obstacles and setbacks are inevitable. Being flexible and resilient allows you to adjust your approach, learn from challenges, and keep moving forward. The ability to adapt ensures that you're not easily derailed by unforeseen circumstances.

4. Continuous Learning: Growth requires a commitment to learning. Whether through formal education, self-study, or real-world experience, expanding your knowledge and skills opens new opportunities and solutions. Lifelong learners are always evolving.

5. Positive Mindset and Self-Belief: Your mindset plays a critical role in progress. Cultivate a positive attitude, believe in your abilities, and maintain self-confidence. Optimism fuels perseverance, and belief in your potential powers your journey toward success.

Perseverance

This is the sustained effort to do your tasks or achieve your goals despite difficulties, failures, or delays. This, like every other attribute, does not come with birth. It is a cultivated skill that is strengthened by adversity (James 1:12). Your perseverance efforts will refine your character and make your life journey a transformative one.

Perseverance is the relentless drive to push forward, even in the face of adversity, setbacks, or delays. It's the unwavering commitment to your tasks and goals, no matter how steep the challenges may appear. This attribute doesn't come naturally or by birth—like a muscle, it must be trained and honed through experience. Adversity is its greatest teacher, for through hardship, perseverance strengthens and takes root deep within you. As James 1:12 reminds us, "Blessed is the one who perseveres under trial, because, having stood the test, that person will receive the crown of life."

Every time you rise after falling, every time you push through the storm, you're chiseling away at the old version of yourself and becoming someone stronger, wiser, and more resilient. Your perseverance not only refines your character, it transforms your entire journey, turning struggles into stepping stones toward greatness. Each trial becomes an opportunity for growth, each failure a lesson in endurance. The key is not in avoiding difficulty, but in facing it head-on and allowing it to shape you into the person you are destined to become. Perseverance, then, is more than just grit—it is the catalyst for a life of meaning, growth, and ultimate success.

Discernment

Simply put, this is the ability to judge well. It can be achieved through the understanding and critical analysis of events or details. This is particularly important because you live in an ever-changing world where many things compete for your attention, tempting you to follow divergent paths. Discernment will come in handy to steer you in the right direction (Proverbs 1:7). This attribute is sharpened by developing a close relationship with God, praying, and meditating on God's word. Also, having a deep reservoir of knowledge will help your discernment efforts.

Courage

It will help you successfully navigate your life journey. It is the ability to confront unpleasant situations without fear of intimidation (Deuteronomy 31:6). A courageous man does not mind swimming against the tide. They take the bull of life by the horns and do what they need to do to make progress. He will press on in spite of all odds. It will take spiritual, mental, moral, and emotional resilience to achieve your goals.

Courage is the guiding force that empowers you to successfully navigate the unpredictable waves of life's journey. It is the ability to face challenges, no matter how daunting, without allowing fear or intimidation to hold you back. As Deuteronomy 31:6 boldly declares, "Be strong and courageous. Do not be afraid or terrified... for the Lord your God goes with you." True courage is rooted in this deep-seated faith, knowing that no matter how difficult the road, you are never walking alone.

A courageous person does not shrink from discomfort or avoid unpleasant situations. Instead, they confront these moments head-on, with conviction and purpose. They are willing to swim against the tide, even when the current of life is powerful and relentless. They do not simply endure—they thrive by taking life's challenges by the horns, refusing to be sidelined by obstacles. Courage is not the absence of fear but the refusal to let fear dictate your actions.

In the face of adversity, courage demands resilience—spiritual, mental, moral, and emotional. To achieve your goals and overcome life's inevitable obstacles, you must cultivate the strength to press on, despite the odds. Mental fortitude allows you to remain focused when doubt creeps in. Emotional resilience keeps your heart steady when disappointment strikes. Moral courage holds you to your principles when temptation sways you from your path. And spiritual courage, perhaps the most vital of all, keeps your soul anchored in faith when everything around you seems uncertain.

Courage transforms ordinary people into extraordinary achievers. It is the inner force that pushes you beyond the limits of comfort, compels you to face the unknown, and enables you to keep moving forward, no matter how fierce the storm. With courage as your companion, you are not only equipped to survive life's challenges—you are destined to rise above them.

Humility

This is the absence of pride. A humble man knows that he is not better placed than others (Philippians 2:3-11). It is not thinking less of yourself, but thinking of yourself less. You love yourself enough to care about yourself, yet you are not self-absorbed. Deeply settled in your spirit is the knowledge that you are who you are by the grace of God. This feeling is prompted by the knowledge that you are who you are by the grace of God.

Humility is the quiet strength that comes with the absence of pride. It is the grace of recognizing that, despite your achievements or status, you are no better than anyone else. As Philippians 2:3-11 teaches, "Do nothing out of selfish ambition or vain conceit. Rather, in humility value others above yourselves." Humility is not about diminishing your worth; it is about understanding your true value without the need to elevate yourself above others.

True humility lies in the balance between self-love and selflessness. You care for and respect yourself, but you are not consumed by the need for recognition or validation. It's not thinking less of yourself, but rather thinking of yourself less—placing the needs and perspectives of others before your own when the moment calls for it. This doesn't mean you neglect your well-being; it means you understand that life is not about you alone.

At the heart of humility is the deep, spiritual knowledge that you are who you are by the grace of God. Everything you have and everything you are stems from His hand. Your talents, opportunities, and even your ability to make progress come from a source greater than yourself. This awareness grounds you and frees you from the chains of arrogance, allowing you to walk through life with quiet confidence. You know that no matter how far you go, the glory belongs to God.

Humility is also the foundation of true leadership and greatness. It allows you to learn from others, admit when you are wrong, and grow without the fear of being seen as less. The humble man is not weakened by his humility—he is empowered by it. He understands that lifting others up, acknowledging their contributions, and creating space for shared success builds a legacy far greater than anything pride can achieve. In humility, you find the strength to serve others, lead with grace, and live a life that reflects the beauty of God's grace upon you.

Adaptability

This is the ability to adjust to different life situations. Life is dynamic, and things keep changing. Sometimes we may need to accommodate people we are not used to or particularly fond of. The ability to adapt will make you more agreeable and help you stay focused (1 Corinthians 10:33). People with adaptable skills are able to manage difficult situations before they reach their breaking point. Flexibility and elasticity are some of their characteristics.

The Power of Identity: Knowing Who You Are

Your identity should not be defined by societal standards, personal achievements, people's endorsements, or otherwise. You should gauge your identity based on how God sees you. Knowing who you are is a revolutionary process that transcends cultural norms and societal expectations. It defines your identity and totally changes how you see yourself. This should be grounded in an understanding of how God perceives you.

In a world that often defines identity by external metrics, this chapter invites you to anchor your sense of self in being a beloved child of God. It is a paradigm shift from being a man pleaser to becoming one who delights in the validation of his creator. Grasping the power of knowing who you are in God's eyes, unlocks your potential in amazing ways. Your confidence, sense of purpose, and self-worth get a boost.

Several biblical characters experienced the transformative power of knowing their identity in God. They were able to overcome identity crisis and inferiority complex. Gideon, the least in his family, emerged as a mighty warrior when he embraced his identity as a valiant hero. Mary Magdalene, liberated from the chains of societal judgment, found a new identity as a devoted follower of Christ. The Samaritan woman at the well, laboring under the burden of a stained reputation, discovered a renewed identity as a messenger of the gospel (John 4:1-25).

In the journey of progress, your identity becomes the lens through which you perceive challenges, setbacks, and victories. It is a source of resilience that withstands the storms of life and a wellspring of confidence that propels you to your destiny. Knowing who you are in God's eyes helps you to anchor your life to what really matters. You are empowered to embrace your role as a candidate for progress.

You are not merely a bystander in the story of progress. You are the protagonist, the candidate chosen for a purpose that will outlive you. Standing on this foundation, fortified and empowered, you are poised to ascend into a life of divine progress.

CHAPTER 2

FAITH IN ACTION

Faith, which is powered by actions (James 2:17), is a dynamic force that propels you into uncharted territories. It is the catalyst that transforms dreams into reality, trials into triumphs, and challenges into opportunities. Faith beckons you to step beyond the realm of theoretical living to engage in a life of the practical application of it. The life of faith is one of courage, overcoming trials, and employing divine strategies to foil the attempts of the enemy. The transformative power of faith in the journey of progress is laid out in this chapter.

Courageous Steps: Walking the Path of Faith
The journey of progress begins with a single step of courage. A popular Chinese proverb says that "the journey of a thousand miles begins with a single step." Taking courageous steps is a walk of faith. This journey invites you to embark on a journey that requires boldness and unwavering trust in your maker. The Bible, a timeless guidebook for the faithful, is replete with stories of individuals who, by taking courageous steps, left indelible marks in the sands of time.

Abraham, the father of faith, lived daringly in Genesis 12:1-4. Our emphasis is on verse 4.

> "[1]Now the Lord said to Abram, 'Go from your
> country and your kindred and your father's
> house to the land that I will show you. [2]And I
> will make of you a great nation, and I will bless

you and make your name great, so that you will
be a blessing. ³ I will bless those who bless you,
and him who dishonors you I will curse, and in
you, all the families of the earth shall be
blessed.' ⁴ So Abram went, as the Lord had told
him...."

Abram, later called Abraham, responded to the divine call with remarkable courage. He left the familiarity of his homeland to venture into an unknown territory, solely relying on the promises of God.

This action was not simply a change of location. It was a demonstration of faith in action. Like Abraham, we are called to take courageous steps, stepping beyond our comfort zones and trusting in the divine guidance that leads to progress.

Triumph Over Trials: Turning Challenges into Opportunities

Trials and challenges are certain companions on the journey of progress. Going through challenges, as Christians, should reframe our perspective of adverse circumstances. We should be prepared to turn them into life-changing opportunities. The Bible is a treasury of wisdom that teaches us to view our trials as stepping stones to greatness. Consider the words of James 1:2-4.

"²Count it all joy, my brothers, when you meet
trials of various kinds, ³ for you know that the
testing of your faith produces steadfastness. ⁴
And let steadfastness have its full effect, that
you may be perfect and complete, lacking in
nothing.

James challenges us to find joy in the midst of our trials, recognizing that they serve as refining agents for our faith. Rather than allowing challenges to weigh us down, we are encouraged to see them as opportunities for the ultimate manifestation of divine progress. Much like a seed must endure the darkness of the soil to sprout into a mighty tree, our passing through the dark tunnels of trials positions us for unprecedented growth and progress.

Divine Strategies: Navigating Obstacles with Faith

In the maze of progress, obstacles are inevitable. The complexities of our situations require us to employ divine strategies to make meaning out of our lives. This section will help us to understand the procedural aspect of life. The Bible provides us with a wealth of strategic insights that empower us to overcome obstacles and emerge victorious. How to do this is locked in Proverbs 3:5-6.

> "5Trust in the Lord with all your heart, and do
> not lean on your understanding. 6 In all your
> ways acknowledge him, and he will make
> straight your paths.

These verses serve as compasses to help us to trust in the divine rather than relying on our understanding. Divine strategies involve aligning our plans with God's purpose, seeking His guidance through prayer and meditation, and acknowledging His sovereignty in every aspect of our lives. As we employ the use of divine strategies, obstacles are no longer insurmountable. They become opportunities for the manifestation of God's power in our progress.

Transformative Sacrifice: Embracing the Journey of Progress

There is a price tag for progress because it will not happen without sacrifice. Sacrificial living, which calls us to let go of the familiar to embrace the unknown, is a key component of faith in action. The Bible, exemplifying the sacrificial love of Christ, teaches us the transformative power of surrendering to the will of God.

In Romans 12:1-2, the apostle Paul implores us thus:

> "[1] I appeal to you, therefore, brothers, by the mercies of God, to present your bodies as a living sacrifice, holy and acceptable to God, which is your spiritual worship. [2] Do not be conformed to this world, but be transformed by the renewal of your mind, that by testing you may discern what is the will of God, what is good and acceptable and perfect.

Transformative sacrifice involves presenting ourselves as living sacrifices to God. It is an act of worship that transcends ritualistic practices, permeating every aspect of our lives. By embracing transformative sacrifice, we position ourselves for a life that aligns with the divine blueprint of progress.

Victorious Living: Manifesting God's Promises through Faith

Victorious living brings to a climax with our study of faith in action. The Bible is replete with stories of people who lived victoriously through the exercise of their unwavering faith in God. From the Old Testament to the New Testament, the scriptures are a testament to the faith-informed living pattern of those who walked in the assurance of God's promises. God's plans for His children are well laid out in Jeremiah 29:11.

> "¹¹For I know the plans I have for you, declares
> the Lord, plans for welfare and not for evil, to
> give you a future and a hope.

Victorious living is not just an ideal to desire. It is a promise that runs through the length and breadth of God's word. As we align our lives with the promises found in the scriptures, faith becomes the bridge between the present reality and the fulfillment of His promises. A victorious life is marked by confidence in God's faithfulness and an unwavering belief in His promises. In 1 Corinthians 15:57, the apostle Paul declares:

> "⁵⁷But thanks be to God, who gives us the
> victory through our Lord Jesus Christ.

This victory is not a future reality. It is at hand, awaiting our acknowledgment and ultimate manifestation. Victorious living is not a denial of challenges but an affirmation that, through faith, we will overcome every obstacle and emerge triumphant in the journey of progress.

Living victoriously is living progressively. We cannot experience one without the other. They are two sides of the same coin. This is the higher life that God has in mind for His children, and it is our honor to be partakers of it.

7 Basic principles of Faith in action.

Here are seven basic principles of faith in action.

1. Belief Beyond Sight

Faith begins with believing in what you cannot see. As Hebrews 11:1 says, "Faith is the substance of things hoped for, the evidence of things not seen." Faith demands that you trust in the unseen, knowing that God's promises are sure even when they haven't yet materialized. This belief is a powerful force, allowing you to step into the unknown with confidence, knowing that the spiritual reality is greater than what your eyes perceive. True faith walks forward, even when the path isn't clear.

2. Confidence in God's Promises

When you act in faith, you're not relying on your own abilities, but on the promises of God. You stand firm, trusting that He who began a good work in you will be faithful to complete it. This principle empowers you to make bold moves, knowing that God's word never returns void. Your confidence in His promises allows you to stay steady in the storm and courageous in the face of obstacles, knowing that the outcome is in His hands.

3. Obedience in Action

Faith is not passive; it calls for action. James 2:17 teaches us that "faith without works is dead." You prove your faith by what you do, not just by what you believe. Acting in faith requires obedience— even when the path seems difficult or the instruction unclear. It's stepping out, trusting that God's direction is right, and knowing that every act of obedience strengthens your faith and aligns you with His will.

4. Persistence Through Trials

Faith is often refined through trials. When circumstances challenge you, it's your persistence that reveals the depth of your faith. Like gold being refined in fire, adversity purifies your trust in God. As James 1:3 reminds us, "The testing of your faith produces perseverance." Trials are not meant to break you; they are designed to build resilience and trust, transforming your struggles into testimonies of God's faithfulness.

5. Speaking Life and Victory

Faith is declared through your words. Proverbs 18:21 tells us that "death and life are in the power of the tongue." The way you speak reflects your faith. When you declare victory, healing, and breakthrough, you align your words with the promises of God. Faith-filled words have the power to shift circumstances, ignite hope, and activate the spiritual realm. Speaking life demonstrates your trust in God's ability to bring His promises to fruition.

6. Surrendering Control

At the core of faith is surrender. It's the willingness to let go of your need for control and trust that God's plan is better than your own. Faith in action means releasing your worries, knowing that His ways are higher. When you surrender your plans to God, you're making room for Him to work in ways that surpass your understanding. It's in surrender that you find true peace, as you rest in the assurance that God's timing and purpose are perfect.

7. Gratitude in Advance

A key principle of faith in action is thanking God before the blessing arrives. Faith says, "I believe it's already done." Gratitude in advance demonstrates your trust that God is at work, even if you don't yet see the results. When you thank God in faith, you shift your focus from what's lacking to what's possible, unleashing the power of expectation. Your gratitude becomes the evidence of things hoped for, and it magnifies God's ability to move on your behalf.

Each of these principles requires trust, action, and a deep connection to God's promises. Faith isn't just something you believe; it's something you live—a daily, active pursuit that draws you closer to God's purpose and unlocks the extraordinary in your life.

CHAPTER 3

EMBRACING GROWTH

Although they have different meanings, growth and progress have been used interchangeably. The former speaks to increase, while the latter speaks to onward movement and betterment. The two are to be desired. The fact that we are growing does not necessarily mean that we are making progress. Chances are quite high, though, that when we are making progress, we are growing.

Growth refers to an increase—whether in knowledge, strength, or capacity—while progress speaks to onward movement and improvement. The two are undoubtedly connected, but they are not the same. You can grow without necessarily advancing, accumulating experiences, or knowledge without making tangible steps forward. However, when you are truly making progress, you are very likely growing, as each step forward demands a deeper understanding, sharper skills, and a refined character.

Growth is foundational; it builds the strength and capability needed to handle greater responsibilities and opportunities. Yet growth, without movement or purpose, can become stagnant. It's like a tree with deep roots but no new branches—it may survive, but it is not flourishing. Progress, on the other hand, pushes you forward. It compels you to take action, to pursue a higher calling, and to move toward the fulfillment of your God-given potential. Progress is not just about doing more—it's about becoming more.

The distinction between growth and progress is essential because we often mistake one for the other. A person may be gaining knowledge, wisdom, or resources (growth), but unless they are applying these gains in meaningful ways, they are not making progress. True progress requires you to move beyond preparation and into action—to take the steps that align with your purpose and advance God's plan for your life. Growth equips you; progress fulfills you.

This chapter invites you to engage in both growth and progress intentionally, understanding that each has a unique role in your journey. Growth enriches your capacity, while progress ensures that this capacity is directed toward your divine calling. Together, they form the path to a life that not only flourishes but also fulfills the purpose for which you were created.

God's mandate for your life is not just about reaching goals; it's about constant transformation. Every experience, every challenge, and every opportunity for growth is a step toward realizing the bigger picture He has set before you. By actively seeking growth, you develop the wisdom, skills, and character needed for the journey. By embracing progress, you take bold steps forward in faith, moving closer to the vision He has for you.

In this chapter, you are encouraged to pursue not only the accumulation of knowledge and strength but also the forward momentum that comes with taking action. This is how you fulfill God's mandate—by growing in His grace and progressing in His purpose, one step at a time. The combination of growth and progress creates a life that is not only abundant but also impactful, radiating God's glory through every milestone and advancement. It is a life that does not just increase but moves upward and onward, always striving to fulfill the divine calling that rests on your shoulders.

Seasons of Progress: Understanding the Divine Timeline
The journey of growth unfolds in distinct seasons, each with its own rhythm and purpose. The concept of divine timing is in tandem with seasons of progress. We understand that our lives are not solely under our control. Rather, there is a designer at work, harmonizing all aspects of our lives to conform to His will. Deep insight is shared in Ecclesiastes 3:1.

> "[1]For everything, there is a season, and a time
> for every matter under heaven.

Understanding the divine timeline requires a discerning heart and a patient spirit. As the farmer awaits the appointed time for planting, he knows that harvesting efforts should be reserved for the pre-determined seasons. The determinant is God. It is a recognition that every season – sowing, waiting, reaping, or resting, all play crucial roles in the symphony of progress.

As we navigate through our seasons, let us embrace the words in Galatians 6:9.

> "[9]And let us not grow weary of doing good, for
> in due season we will reap, if we do not give up.

This verse provides encouragement to persevere, trusting that, in the divine timeline, our efforts will bear fruit at the appointed hour.

Fruitful Harvest: Cultivating a Life of Abundance

The journey of growth is more than mere existence. It is a call to be fruitful. While not everything that grows is healthy, all healthy organisms grow. Cancers, fibroids, etc. grow, but they do not depict good health. However, when healthy organisms grow, they mature and ultimately yield fruits. This section explores the principle of sowing and reaping in the process of progress. It is a divine economy where the seeds we plant determine the harvest we reap.

"7Do not be deceived: God is not mocked, for
whatever one sows, that will he also reap.

Galatians 6:7

The fertile soil of our hearts, when nourished with faith, love, and positive actions, becomes the fertile soil for a bountiful harvest. The fruits we bear are not only for our consumption but are meant to be a blessing to those around us. As we cultivate a life of abundance, we become conduits of divine generosity, reflecting the character of the one who provides abundantly.

"23As for what was sown on good soil, this is the
one who hears the word and understands it. He
indeed bears fruit and yields, in one case a
hundredfold, in another sixty, and in another
thirty.

Matthew 13:23:

The fertile soil of a receptive heart yields a harvest that exceeds expectations. This is a testament to the transformative power of cultivating a life of abundance.

Renewed Mindset: Breaking Chains for Personal Growth

True growth goes beyond the externals. It takes place inside us and finds expression outside. A renewed mindset breaks the chains of limiting beliefs and embraces the limitless potential within. This section explores the transformative power of the mind, leveraging Romans 12:2.

> "2Do not be conformed to this world, but be
> transformed by the renewal of your mind, that
> by testing you may discern what is the will of
> God, what is good and acceptable and perfect.

Breaking chains for personal growth is an intentional shift from a mindset of scarcity to one of abundance, from fear to faith, and from self-limitation to self-actualization. It requires a conscious effort to align our thoughts with the words in Philippians 4:13, which say we can do all things through the strength of Christ.

Let us take a cue from the story of Caleb in Joshua 14:10-12. Despite the presence of giants in the promised land, Caleb possessed a different spirit because he followed the Lord. His mindset of faith and confidence in God's promises positioned him to surmount all difficulties. Similarly, a renewed mindset empowers us to conquer the mountains in our lives, paving the way for personal growth and development.

Divine Gardening: Nurturing Seeds of Progress

To nurture the seeds of progress in us, we have to engage in divine gardening. The requirements for natural gardening include sunlight, water, seeds, farming implements, etc. Divine gardening is an intentional spiritual exercise. It is a recognition that the seeds of progress require nourishment through prayer, meditation, and alignment with divine principles. As a diligent gardener tends to the needs of the soil, we, too, must be attentive to the spiritual, mental, and emotional aspects of our lives.

The smallest seed ever, the mustard seed, is used to teach us a lesson in Matthew 13:31-32.

> "³¹The kingdom of heaven is like a grain of
> mustard seed that a man took and sowed in his
> field. ³² It is the smallest of all seeds, but when it
> has grown, it is larger than all the garden plants
> and becomes a tree, so that the birds of the air
> come and make nests in its branches.

Divine gardening transforms seemingly small seeds of potential into towering trees of progress, providing shelter and nourishment for those around them.

Thriving in Adversity: Flourishing Amidst Challenges
Adversity, though usually perceived as a hindrance, becomes a crucible for growth when viewed through the lens of faith. Much of the good we attain in our lives emanates from seasons of intense stress. Here, we will examine the resilience required to flourish in the face of life's storms. James 1:2-4 reminds us to view our trials differently.

> "²Count it all joy, my brothers, when you meet
> trials of various kinds, ³for you know that the
> testing of your faith produces steadfastness.
> ⁴And let steadfastness have its full effect, that
> you may be perfect and complete, lacking in
> nothing.

Maintaining that you can thrive in adversity is not a denial of the stifling effects of challenges. Rather, it is an affirmation that, through faith, we can navigate the storms and emerge stronger on the other side. Like trees firmly planted by the water in Jeremiah 17:7-8.

After facing betrayal, slavery, and imprisonment, Joseph thrived in adversity. His unwavering faith allowed him to survive, flourish, and eventually become the solution to the problems of his people. Thriving in adversity is a testament to the transformative power of growth amidst challenges.

Your journey of growth is not a solitary exercise. It is a step-by-step walk with the divine. You should see to it that your hands are firmly grasped by Him as He walks you on the path of progress.

Here are 8 powerful ways to harness growth and progress, each with insights to inspire you along your journey:

1. Embrace a Growth Mindset

To harness growth and progress, you must first embrace the belief that your abilities can be developed. This is what renowned psychologist Carol Dweck calls a "growth mindset." Instead of viewing challenges as threats, see them as opportunities for growth. A growth mindset empowers you to push beyond your limits, knowing that failures are not the end but stepping stones toward success. With the right mindset, every setback becomes a setup for a greater comeback.

2. Set Clear, Purpose-Driven Goals

Growth and progress are intentional. Without clear goals, you can easily wander through life without direction. Set goals that are aligned with your purpose and vision. When your goals are driven by purpose, they serve as a compass, guiding your efforts and keeping you motivated. Break these goals down into actionable steps, and you'll not only grow in capacity but also steadily progress toward fulfilling your mission.

3. Cultivate Lifelong Learning

True growth is a continuous journey. Commit to being a lifelong learner—whether through formal education, reading, experiences, or mentorship. The more you learn, the more you equip yourself to face new challenges and seize new opportunities. Learning doesn't just increase your knowledge—it expands your mind and enhances your ability to progress in every area of life. Knowledge opens doors; wisdom helps you walk through them.

4. Take Consistent Action

Progress is born out of consistent effort. It's not enough to have big dreams—you must take daily steps to move closer to them. Small, intentional actions compound over time, leading to significant advancements. Growth without action is stagnant, but progress is made by doing, even if it's one step at a time. Consistency transforms potential into reality, turning dreams into accomplishments.

5. Build Resilience

Both growth and progress require resilience. Along the journey, you will face setbacks, criticism, and failures. However, it's your ability to bounce back that determines your success. Resilience is the strength to keep going when things get tough. Every obstacle you face is an opportunity to grow stronger, wiser, and more determined. In adversity, you don't just survive—you thrive, because you know that each challenge refines and prepares you for the next level.

6. Seek Out Mentorship and Feedback

You don't have to grow or progress alone. Surround yourself with mentors, coaches, and people who can provide constructive feedback. A mentor accelerates your growth by sharing wisdom from their own experiences, helping you avoid pitfalls, and guiding you toward greater progress. At the same time, feedback from others gives you the perspective you might not have. When you remain teachable and open to advice, you fast-track your development.

7. Celebrate Small Wins

Acknowledging your progress is crucial for maintaining momentum. Don't wait until you've reached the final goal to celebrate—take time to appreciate the small wins along the way. Each step forward, no matter how small, is proof that you're growing and moving closer to your desired outcome. Celebrating these moments boosts your motivation and reminds you of how far you've come. Progress is a journey, and each victory fuels the next step.

8. Stay Connected to Your Purpose

The most powerful way to harness growth and progress is by staying deeply connected to your purpose. When you are aligned with God's calling for your life, every action you take holds meaning. Your purpose gives your growth direction and your progress significance. It helps you see beyond the present challenges and fuels you with passion to keep pressing forward. When your purpose drives you, nothing can stop you, because you're not just progressing for yourself—you're fulfilling a divine mandate.

Incorporating these principles into your life will ensure that both your growth and progress are intentional, consistent, and aligned with your higher calling. By adopting a growth mindset, setting purposeful goals, staying resilient, and taking consistent action, you create a powerful momentum that propels you forward. Seek mentorship, learn continuously, celebrate every milestone, and always keep your purpose in sight.

Growth transforms you, and progress elevates you—both are essential for leading a life of significance and impact. When you harness the power of growth and progress, you unlock your potential and step boldly into the life God has designed for you.

CHAPTER 4

PARTNERING WITH THE DIVINE

Our partnership with the divine is the key that unlocks the fullness of our potential. *Partnering with the Divine* calls us to collaboration with God. It invites us to a relationship characterized by prayerful progress, divine co-labouring, miraculous guidance, tapping into heavenly resources, and unleashing the transformative power of divine empowerment. When we collaborate or synergize with God, we are sure to have better life outcomes. We, on a progressive basis, become better versions of ourselves.

This partnership is not passive; it calls us to be active participants in the unfolding of God's plans for our lives. It's a dynamic relationship where our faith and God's power intersect to create miraculous outcomes.

Prayerful Progress: Communicating with the Divine
At the center of our partnership with God lies the transformative practice of prayer. Divine progress is impossible for the believer without prayers. Engaging the agency of prayers show that our dependency is on God. Regular dialogue with your creator invites peace and tranquility into our lives. We are empowered to minister to people because it is unusual to find peace in the midst of troubles. Philippians 4:6-7 gives a clear perspective on the matter.

> "⁶Do not be anxious about anything, but in
> everything by prayer and supplication with
> thanksgiving let your requests be made known to

God. ⁷And the peace of God, which surpasses all
understanding, will guard your hearts and your
minds in Christ Jesus.

Prayerful progress is the surrender of our fears, hopes, and dreams into the hands of the Divine. It is an acknowledgment that, in the act of prayer, we align our will to that of God, inviting His transformative power into every aspect of our lives. The words of Jesus Christ in Luke 22:40-42 are ones many Christians are not keen to repeat.

"⁴⁰And when he was at the place, he said unto
them, Pray that ye enter not into temptation.
⁴¹And he was withdrawn from them about a
stone's cast, and kneeled down, and prayed,
⁴² Saying, Father, if thou be willing, remove this
cup from me: nevertheless not my will, but
thine, be done.

Prayer is an intimate communion that bears fruit in the open arenas of our lives.

Daniel, despite his challenges, maintained a disciplined practice of prayer, trusting in God's guidance. His unwavering commitment to prayer not only secured him divine protection but also positioned him for unparalleled progress and influence in a foreign land.

Our prayers, arising from a righteous heart, have the power to transform circumstances and usher in a season of divine progress.

Divine Co-Laborers: Your Partnership with God
Our partnership with God involves other aspects apart from prayer. It is a collaborative relationship where we actively

participate in the divine narrative. As divine co-laborers, we understand that we are not mere spectators but active contributors to the unfolding story of progress. In 1 Corinthians 3:9, the Apostle Paul tells us the divine role we occupy.

> "⁹For we are God's fellow workers. You are
> God's field, God's building.

This partnership involves aligning our efforts with God's purposes. It is a recognition that, as co-laborers, our efforts are not in vain. Just as a farmer works on the field with the expectation of a harvest, we engage in our tasks with the anticipation of divine fruitfulness.

The relationship between the potter and the clay is one that artists, artisans, and indeed many of us are familiar with. Isaiah 64:8 tells us we are God's handiwork.

In this partnership, God is not only the master architect but also the skilled artisan, shaping and molding us into vessels of honor. As we actively participate in the divine process, progress becomes a collaborative venture between the creator and the created.

Noah's life serves as an inspiring example of divine collaboration. Before the flood, Noah obediently followed God's instructions, building the ark that would ensure the preservation of mankind. His partnership with God not only secured his family's safety but also marked a new beginning for humanity.

Philippians 2:13 talks about our partnership with God.

"[13]For it is God who works in you, both to will
and to work for his good pleasure.

A harmonious synergy, where our desires align with His will, ensues.

Miraculous Guidance: Using the Divine Navigation System

The intricacies and complexities of life necessitate that we have divine guidance. Without it, we are bound to lose our way. The divine navigation system is a supernatural guidance system that directs our steps along the path of progress. It, unlike natural navigation systems, is always accurate. Proverbs 3:5-6 has this to say about trusting God.

"[5]Trust in the Lord with all your heart, and do
not lean on your understanding. [6]In all your
ways acknowledge him, and he will make
straight your paths.

Trusting the divine navigation system involves surrendering our limited understanding to the omniscient wisdom of God. It is an acknowledgment that God sees the entire picture, while we merely perceive fragments. Much like a ship relies on a navigation system to traverse vast oceans, we entrust our journey to the guidance of the divine navigator.

The Israelites, in the wilderness, were guided by a pillar of cloud by day, and a pillar of fire illuminated their path by night. Divine guidance is a warm reminder that God will never leave nor forsake us. We know He has our backs and will ensure that we do not get lost in the maze of life.

In Psalm 119:105, the word of God guides us on our journey of progress. The Word of God serves as a light and a lamp.

The former illuminates our immediate steps, and the latter glows to cast a light on the broader dimensions of our lives. In moments of uncertainty, the divine navigation system becomes our source of confidence and assurance.

Heavenly Resources: Tapping into God's Abundance
Our partnership with God gives us access to heavenly resources – a wellspring of abundance that surpasses earthly limitations. We serve a God of abundance and not of scarcity. Inexhaustible treasures are available to all who trust in God. Anytime you have a need, remind yourself that there is more where your needs are met. It never runs dry. We read this in Philippians 4:19.

> "19And my God will supply every need of yours
> according to his riches in glory in Christ Jesus.

Tapping into God's abundance involves a shift in mentality from scarcity to sufficiency. We acknowledge that, as co-heirs with Christ, we inherit the riches of God's glory. Just as a branch draws nourishment from the vine, we access heavenly resources through our intimate connection with the divine source.

The widow at Zarephath in 1 Kings 17:12-16, in the midst of a severe famine, trusted the divine guidance of Elijah. She witnessed the miraculous multiplication of her meager resources. Her obedience and faith opened the door to heavenly abundance, providing sustenance not only for herself, but for Elijah as well.

The inexhaustibility of our source is presented in Ephesians 3:20. The abundance of God transcends our limited expectations, inviting us to dream and believe for more provision in the journey of progress.

Divine Empowerment: Unleashing God's Power for Progress

In the realm of divine partnership, empowerment becomes a transformative force that propels us beyond our natural capacities. Divine empowerment is possible through the agency of the Holy Spirit. This section shows us how to be empowered by the divine to overcome obstacles and fulfill our purpose. Acts 1:8 tells us how to acquire spiritual power.

> "⁸But you will receive power when the Holy
> Spirit has come upon you, and you will be my
> witnesses in Jerusalem and in all Judea and
> Samaria, and to the end of the earth.

Divine empowerment is not meant to be accessed in the future. It is a present reality accessible through the indwelling presence of the Holy Spirit. It involves a surrender to the transformative power that equips us for the challenges and opportunities presented in the journey of progress. As we unleash God's power within us, we become witnesses of His glory, testifying to God's transformative work in our lives.

David, in facing Goliath, is a worthy example. Empowered by faith and trust in God, he overcame an insurmountable challenge, showcasing the transformative power of divine empowerment. His victory was not rooted in human strength but in the empowering presence of the divine.

Divine empowerment dispels fear, infuses us with power, envelops us in love, and grants us the self-control needed for a disciplined and purposeful life (2 Timothy 1:7).

Miraculous Guidance

One of the most powerful benefits of partnering with the Divine is the access to miraculous guidance. God's wisdom far surpasses human understanding, and when we walk in partnership with Him, we are led by His perfect knowledge. This guidance opens doors that no man can shut and makes ways where there seems to be no way. It's the miracle of being in the right place at the right time, receiving the right opportunities, and experiencing breakthroughs that only God could orchestrate. With divine guidance, our paths are illuminated, and our steps are sure, leading to better life outcomes.

Becoming Better Versions of Ourselves

Through this divine synergy, we are continually refined and improved. Each day, as we walk with God, we are shaped by His Spirit, becoming more like Him—more compassionate, more wise, more resilient. Progressive transformation is a hallmark of partnering with the Divine. We don't remain stagnant; instead, we are ever-evolving, becoming better versions of ourselves in every area of life. As we embrace His will and purpose, we grow in character, capacity, and spiritual maturity. Partnering with God ensures that we are not only moving forward in life but growing into the fullness of who He created us to be.

Better Life Outcomes

Ultimately, partnering with God leads to better life outcomes. When we collaborate with the Divine, we can expect a life marked by peace, purpose, and fulfillment. We are no longer tossed by the waves of circumstance or confined by human limitations, because we are connected to the One who controls the universe. God's wisdom, power, and resources are at work in us and for us, resulting in outcomes that surpass our wildest expectations. The life that is partnered with God is one that flourishes in every season, bearing fruit that lasts and impacting others in ways that only the divine partnership can achieve.

In this divine partnership, you are not alone. You are walking in step with the Creator, whose plans for you are far greater than you can imagine. When you partner with God, you move from striving to thriving, from limitation to liberation. You harness His power, tap into His resources, and walk in His divine purpose, resulting in a life of extraordinary impact and fulfillment.

CHAPTER 5

LEGACY OF PROGRESS

Our lives echo through the corridors of time, leaving imprints that transcend our earthly sojourn. Everyone leaves an impression after their earthly sojourn. The big question is; What legacy are you leaving? This section explores the knowledge that each step we take and every choice we make contributes to a narrative of enduring impact. As we go through the chapters of eternal impact, inspirational leadership, generational blessings, living stones, and heavenly rewards, may the ageless words of the Bible illuminate the path, inspiring us to build a legacy that resonates with divine progress.

Eternal Impact: Building a Lasting Legacy

A legacy is money or property that someone leaves when they die. Legacies cause our influence to be continually felt long after we are gone. We are invited to contemplate the lasting significance of our actions in the grand narrative of existence. Ecclesiastes 3:11 captures the eternal dimensions of our lives.

> "[11]He has made everything beautiful in its time.
> Also, he has put eternity into man's heart, yet so
> that he cannot find out what God has done from
> the beginning to the end.

Building a lasting legacy involves recognizing that our actions, whether motivated by divine purpose or otherwise, have eternal ramifications. The legacy we leave is not confined to material accomplishments; it touches all areas of life - spiritual, financial, and emotional well-being of those we leave behind. It is intricately woven into the fabric of eternity. As we navigate through the chapters of our lives, let us be mindful of the eternal impact each decision carries.

When we lay up treasure for ourselves in heaven, as indicated in Matthew 6:19-20, we are living a good legacy. Heavenly-minded people live selflessly.

The treasures we accumulate on earth are subject to external forces: natural disasters, fraud, theft, carelessness, government policies, etc. It is only the treasures we lay up for ourselves in heaven that will outlive us. It is from them that we receive our eternal rewards.

Every birthday we mark should be one of reflection. While it is good to celebrate God's goodness to us up until then, it is more important to use the day as a reminder to live more intentionally (Psalm 90:12).

Wisdom guides us to invest our time, talents, and resources in endeavors that outlast the temporal and resonate through eternity. Building a lasting legacy is an intentional journey that requires a heart attuned to the eternal rhythm of divine progress.

Inspirational Leadership: Guiding Others toward Progress

Leadership is not merely occupying a position of authority but a call to inspire and guide others toward progress. The proof that you are a leader is that people follow you. People follow those that have an influence on them. Leadership is influence. This section explores the transformative influence leaders have on those they lead. Proverbs 11:14 talks about the importance of guidance. Unguided people are not likely to live productive and progressive lives.

> "¹⁴Where there is no guidance, a people falls, but in an abundance of counselors, there is safety.

Inspirational leaders are committed to serving and uplifting others. Usually, they instinctively recognize potential in people. The Bible, a treasure trove of leadership principles, showcases leaders who, through their inspirational guidance, steered others toward divine purpose.

Moses, an inspirational leader, led the Israelites through the wilderness to the promised land. His efforts infused hope, courage, and faith into the heart of a nation. His leadership style serves as a workable model for those called to guide others toward progress.

Inspirational leadership is not a function of age or title. It is a function of investment into their lives. This is why young people who are full of wisdom are to admirable. When leaders exemplify progress, they become beacons of light, guiding others to the fulfillment of their destinies.

In Colossians 3:23-24, we hear from the Apostle Paul, who, by the way, was also an inspirational leader. He noted that we will receive an inheritance as our reward as long as we are serving Christ.

Inspirational leadership is a sacred responsibility, undertaken with the understanding that, ultimately, our service is unto the Lord. Our legacies are eternally intertwined with the progress of those we lead.

Generational Blessings: Passing the Torch of Progress
The concept of generational blessings underpins the profound impact of our lives on posterity. Christians must always live with posterity, which refers to all future generations of people, in view. This section invites us to consider the far-reaching effects of our choices. Responsible parents, teachers, mentors, and coaches are keen to die empty. They are deeply motivated by the need to pour their lives into others. Their motto is 'give back.' Psalm 78:4 emphasizes this generational responsibility.

> "⁴We will not hide them from their children, but
> tell to the coming generation the glorious deeds
> of the Lord, and his might, and the wonders that
> he has done.

Passing the torch of progress involves intentional efforts to impart wisdom, values, and a legacy of faith to succeeding generations. Abounding in the Bible are examples of instances where the faithfulness of one generation becomes the foundation for the progress of the next.

Timothy's faith was nurtured by his grandmother, Lois, and his mother, Eunice (2 Timothy 1:5). The generational blessing of faith imparted to Timothy positioned him for impactful ministry alongside the Apostle Paul. This intergenerational transfer of faith and values echoes the responsibility we carry to pass the torch of progress to those who come after us. Parents, leaders, etc. are encouraged to heed the counsel of Proverbs 22:6.

> "⁶Train up a child in the way he should go; even
> when he is old, he will not depart from it.

This proverb encapsulates the essence of intentional parenting and mentorship. We recognize that investment in the spiritual and moral development of the younger generation yields a harvest of progress that endures.

Generational blessings, as indicated above, are not limited to biological relationships. They extend to spiritual, professional, and educational relationships as well. In Titus 2:3-5, Paul instructs older women to teach and mentor younger women. Other mentor/mentee relationships are Jethro and Moses, Moses and Joshua, Eli and Samuel, Elijah and Elisha, Mordecai and Esther, Jesus and His disciples, Barnabas and Paul, and Paul mentoring Timothy.

When the body of Christ prioritizes mentoring, a crop of mature Christians who will be able to administer God's estate is developed.

Living Stones: Constructing a Testament of Divine Progress

Our lives, like stones in a grand edifice, contribute to the construction of a testament that speaks of divine progress. Stones are strong and are major building materials. This section takes its from 1 Peter 2:5.

> "5You yourselves like living stones are being
> built up as a spiritual house, to be a holy
> priesthood, to offer spiritual sacrifices
> acceptable to God through Jesus Christ.

Every choice and act of faith contributes to the construction of a spiritual house – a testament of divine progress that stands as a monument to God's faithfulness. Just as stones are utilized for construction, our lives, when aligned with divine purpose, become part of a divine narrative.

Consider the construction of Solomon's temple in the Old Testament. The meticulous craftsmanship and precision in assembling the stones mirrored the divine order and purpose behind the construction. Similarly, our lives, when in harmony with God's Word, become part of a spiritual edifice that testifies to the transformative power of divine progress.

As living stones, we should be aligned with the cornerstone – Jesus Christ (Ephesians 2:20-22).

The construction of a testament of divine progress involves unity with Christ as the cornerstone and unity with fellow believers. The synchronization of living stones, bound together by the mortar of love and faith, creates a dwelling place for God's presence. Our lives, when lived in harmony with divine principles, become a testament that points others toward the transformative power of God.

Heavenly Rewards: The Culmination of a Life Committed to Progress

The culmination of a life committed to progress is heavenly rewards – a promise that transcends earthly accolades and material gain. We are invited to study heavenly treasures and the eternal significance of a life lived in accordance with divine purpose. Matthew 6:19-21 explains this well.

> "[19]Lay not up for yourselves treasures upon earth, where moth and rust doth corrupt, and where thieves break through and steal: [20]But lay up for yourselves treasures in heaven, where neither moth nor rust doth corrupt, and where thieves do not break through nor steal: [21]For where your treasure is, there will your heart be also.

Heavenly rewards, unlike earthly awards, are not transactional in nature. They reflect the heart's alignment with God's purpose. The Bible abounds with promises of rewards for faithfulness, endurance, and obedience (Revelation 22:12)

The heavenly rewards spoken of in scripture are not limited to material abundance. They encompass the fullness of God's promises, including eternal life, intimate communion with Him, and a share in His glory on earth. As we navigate the chapters of our lives, let us fix our gaze on the eternal rewards that await those who persevere on the journey of progress.

Apostle Paul, in 2 Timothy 4:7-8, boldly states:

> "[7]I have fought the good fight, I have finished the race, I have kept the faith. [8]Henceforth there is laid up for me the crown of righteousness, which the Lord, the righteous judge, will award to me on that day, and not only to me but also to all who have loved his appearing.

The heavenly reward is not only for the Apostle Paul but for all who, like him, have remained faithful to the end.

The benefits accruable to a life committed to divine progress are participation in the unimaginable, glorious, and eternal rewards that surpass the limitations of earthly pursuits.

The legacy of progress is intertwined with eternal impact, inspirational leadership, generational blessings, living stones, and heavenly rewards.

CHAPTER 6

VEHICLES OF A PROGRESSING
CANDIDATE

Life is an adventure. In it, every individual navigates a journey of twists, turns, challenges, and triumphs. To embark on this journey as a progressing candidate is to embrace a dynamic and purposeful approach to life. This chapter, *Vehicles of a Progressing Candidate*, is a roadmap that delves into the essential elements that propel individuals toward their divine destinies. Drawing inspiration from the timeless verses of the Bible, we will explore vehicles that serve as catalysts for progress, urging each candidate to accelerate towards the fulfillment of their purpose.

Faith: The Engine of Progress
At the heart of every progressive candidate lies the powerful engine of faith. When faith is powered by works, we are empowered to tackle the obstacles that are ahead of us. Hebrews 11 provides a rich perspective on the topic of faith.

> "[1]Now faith is the assurance of things hoped for,
> the evidence of things not seen.[2] For by it the
> elders obtained a good report.[3] Through faith we
> understand that the worlds were framed by the
> word of God, so that things which are seen were
> not made of things which do appear.

Faith is the unwavering assurance that, beyond the visible, there exists a realm of promise and possibility. In the realm of faith, 'believing is seeing' as opposed to the regular refrain of 'seeing is believing.' It must be mentioned that faith can be facilitated by sight. This is through the study of apologetics, which is the rational, logical, and physical defense of our faith.

As a progressing candidate, your journey begins with faith – faith in yourself, in the divine purpose intricately woven into your being, and in the one who designs your progress pathways. The engine of faith, fueled by trust and belief, empowers you to navigate through uncertainties and challenges to the fulfillment of your destiny.

Vision: Navigating with Clarity
In the landscape of progress, vision serves as the navigation system, providing clarity and direction. Possessing a vision makes you see beyond the apparent because you possess the power to anticipate events. Proverbs 29:18 says:

> "[18]Where there is no vision, the people perish,
> but he that keepeth the law, happy is he.

A progressing candidate is one who envisions his destination and charts a course that aligns with his divine purpose.

A visionary person cannot sit still because he is propelled to actualize his potential. Vision is the compass that ensures your steps are purposeful and aligned with the overarching plan of God for your life. As a candidate for progress, have a compelling and clear vision for yourself and those you lead.

Determination: Overcoming Every Roadblock
Determination is the fuel that propels the progressing candidate past every roadblock and obstacle. A determined

person is firm and resolute. He is unperturbed by life circumstances. The spirit of determination is captured in Philippians 3:13-14.

> "¹³Brethren, I count not myself to have
> apprehended: but this one thing I do, forgetting
> those things which are behind, and reaching
> forth unto those things which are before, ¹⁴I
> press toward the mark for the prize of the high
> calling of God in Christ Jesus.

Although the journey of progress is fraught with challenges, a determined candidate views every obstacle as an opportunity for growth. He fearlessly fights back in the face of opposition.

Be determined to persevere, recognizing that every setback is a setup for a comeback. It will help you conquer challenges and transform setbacks into stepping stones toward success.

Wisdom: Navigating with Discernment

In the journey of progress, wisdom serves as the discerning navigator, guiding the candidate through complex terrains. Wisdom facilitates thinking. It helps to utilize knowledge, experience, understanding, common sense, and insight. Proverbs 4:7-9 has this to say about wisdom:

> "⁷Wisdom is the principal thing; therefore get
> wisdom: and with all thy getting get
> understanding.⁸ Exalt her, and she shall promote
> thee: she shall bring thee to honour, when thou
> dost embrace her.⁹ She shall give to thine head
> an ornament of grace: a crown of glory shall she
> deliver to thee.

A progressing candidate values the acquisition of wisdom, with the understanding that it is a critical element to making informed decisions.

Wisdom is not merely theoretical knowledge but the practical application of knowledge. It empowers you to navigate through life, assess risks, and make informed decisions that align with divine principles. As a progressing candidate, let wisdom be your constant companion on the journey of progress.

Resilience: Bouncing Back from Setbacks
Resilience is the shock absorber that enables the progressing candidate to bounce back from setbacks and challenges. Resilient people are flexible, so they have the ability to stretch themselves. They know how to find happiness again when something bad has happened to them. James 1:2-4 provides a perspective on resilience.

> "²Count it all joy, my brothers, when you meet
> trials of various kinds, ³for you know that the
> testing of your faith produces steadfastness.
> ⁴And let steadfastness have its full effect, that
> you may be perfect and complete, lacking in
> nothing.

A progressing candidate understands that setbacks are not roadblocks but stepping stones to growth. Cultivate resilience as a core attribute, allowing your challenges to refine and strengthen your character.

Patience: Trusting the Divine Timeline

Patience is the virtue that aligns the progressing candidate with the divine timeline. Patient people do not make haste.

They understand that although it takes so long for trees to grow, ultimately, they provide food, prevent soil erosion, and combat the ill-effects of climate change. Hebrews 6:12 encourages us to be patient.

> "²so that you may not be sluggish but imitators
> of those who through faith and patience inherit
> the promises.

A patiently progressing candidate recognizes that God's timing is perfect and trusts in the unfolding of His promises. A patient man controls himself while waiting. He is mindful not to say or do anything that will undermine his trust in God.

Impatience can lead to detours and hasty decisions, while patience allows for the full maturation of progress. As you navigate your journey, determine to wait on the Lord, confident that His promises will manifest in due time.

Discipline: Cultivating Habits of Success

Discipline serves as the steering wheel that keeps the progressing candidate on the path to success. It takes discipline to turn goals into accomplishments and ideas into great products. Proverbs 13:4 emphasizes the importance of discipline.

> "⁴The soul of the sluggard craves and gets
> nothing, while the soul of the diligent is richly
> supplied.

A progressing candidate understands that success is often the result of consistent and disciplined habits. Breaking bad habits and establishing good ones take time and discipline.

Cultivate a lifestyle of discipline by making intentional choices that contribute to your progress. Whether in your personal development, work, or relationships, discipline ensures that you stay focused on the road ahead.

Humility: Embracing Growth Opportunities

Humility is the quality that keeps the progressing candidate open to growth and receptive to divine guidance. A humble person rates himself with modesty. He refuses to be carried away by his accomplishments. Proverbs 22:4 tells us the reward for humility.

> "4By humility and the fear of the LORD are
> riches, and honour, and life.

A progressive candidate recognizes that humility is not weakness but strength that invites divine favor.

Embrace humility as a key component of your character, acknowledging that there is always room for growth and improvement. A humble candidate seeks wisdom, welcomes feedback, and remains teachable, ensuring that the journey of progress is marked by continuous development.

Gratitude: Fueling Positive Momentum

Gratitude serves as the fuel that provides the progressing candidate with positive momentum. A grateful person is thankful for the blessings he receives from God. In his estimation, nothing is too small to be thankful for. 1 Thessalonians 5:18 says:

> "18Give thanks in all circumstances; for this is
> the will of God in Christ Jesus for you.

A progressive candidate understands the power of gratitude in shaping his life outcomes.

Cultivate an attitude of gratitude by recognizing the blessings and opportunities on your journey. Gratitude fuels optimism, resilience, and a sense of abundance.

Grateful people are healthy people. Having a grateful heart keeps your mind alert, making you ready to kick off the day on a good note.

Generosity: Sharing the Wealth of Progress

Generosity is the open window through which the progressing candidate shares his wealth of progress with others. A generous person not only shares his money. He willingly rations everything that God blesses him with: time, resources, wisdom, etc. Proverbs 11:25 shows us the benefits of generosity.

> "25The liberal soul shall be made fat: and he that
> watereth shall be watered also himself.

A progressive candidate understands that true wealth is not only for personal gain but for the benefit of others as well. It opens its nest for others to take shelter in.

Make your life a conduit for God's blessings. As you look out for the well-being of others, you create a positive ripple effect that enhances the overall progress of your community. Generosity is not only a virtue. It is a powerful vehicle that accelerates the journey of progress.

Adaptability: Navigating Through Change

Adaptability is the versatile vehicle that allows the progressing candidate to navigate through the inevitable changes of life. It measures whether we react or respond to change. Adaptable people are able to make new connections should the need arise.

> "Just as I try to please everyone in everything I
> do, not seeking my own advantage, but that of
> many, that they may be saved.
>
> 1 Corinthians 10:33
> "

A progressing candidate understands that change is a constant companion on his life journey.

Adaptability allows you to pivot when necessary, learn from new experiences, and thrive in adverse situations. The ability to adapt ensures that you remain agile on the road of progress, turning challenges into opportunities for growth.

Love: The Fuel of Divine Progress

Love is the transcendent fuel that provides the progressing candidate with divine momentum. A person who walks in love knows that he will amount to nothing in God's kingdom without love. 1 Corinthians 13:2 articulates the significance of love.

> "[2]And though I have the gift of prophecy, and
> understand all mysteries, and all knowledge; and
> though I have all faith, so that I could remove
> mountains, and have not charity, I am nothing.

Love is the essence of divine progress. It infuses every aspect of the journey with purpose and meaning. Let it be the driving force behind your actions, decisions, and interactions. Love for God, oneself, and others infuses every step with purpose. It is this divine quality that will keep you focused on your journey of progress. It transforms this journey into a sacred pilgrimage, where every milestone is marked by the profound impact of love.

Measuring your progress

For we stretch not ourselves beyond our measure, as though we reached not unto you: for we are come as far as to you also in preaching the gospel of Christ: 2 Corinthians 10:14.

Measuring your progress is a powerful practice that enables you to stay on course, celebrate victories, and adjust when needed. It's not just about tracking achievements, but about understanding your journey and how each step moves you closer to your purpose. By regularly assessing where you stand, you turn vague aspirations into tangible outcomes. You don't just guess at your growth—you see it, feel it, and own it.

1. Clarity Brings Focus

Measuring your progress begins with clarity. You can't measure what you haven't defined. When you set clear goals, you create a roadmap for your journey. This clarity brings focus, ensuring that every step you take is purposeful and aligned with your greater vision. Knowing where you are going gives you the power to chart your path, and measuring your progress keeps you focused on the destination.

2. Celebrating Milestones Fuels Motivation

Every small victory deserves recognition. When you measure your progress, you create opportunities to celebrate how far you've come. These celebrations—whether they're big or small—fuel your motivation. They remind you that you're not standing still, that every effort is contributing to something greater. Success is not a single event; it's the accumulation of consistent, intentional actions. Each milestone, no matter how small, is a testament to your growth and commitment.

3. Feedback Strengthens Growth

Measuring progress also provides feedback, helping you see what's working and what's not. It's a mirror that reflects the truth about your journey. This feedback is invaluable because it allows you to adjust your approach, refine your strategy, and strengthen your resolve. Growth without feedback is like planting a seed without tending to it—it won't thrive. Regularly evaluating your progress ensures that you are continually learning and improving, moving forward with greater wisdom.

4. Keeps You Accountable

Accountability is a key to progress. When you measure your progress, you hold yourself accountable to your goals. This accountability pushes you to stay committed, even when the journey gets tough. It's easy to lose sight of your vision when you're not tracking your steps. But when you measure where you are, you stay grounded in the reality of what still needs to be done. Measuring progress keeps you honest, reminding you that you're responsible for your growth and success.

5. Adjusting Your Course with Wisdom

Life is full of unexpected turns, and sometimes, your initial plans need adjustment. Measuring progress allows you to pivot when necessary. It's not about rigidly sticking to a plan that no longer serves you; it's about using the data of your experience to make informed decisions. If something isn't working, you can shift strategies, knowing that you're still moving forward. Progress isn't a straight line—it's a journey of adaptation, learning, and refining your path as you grow.

6. Turning Effort into Achievement

We often put in effort but wonder if it's making a difference. Measuring your progress bridges the gap between effort and achievement. When you measure your actions, you can see how each effort contributes to your overall success. This transforms hard work from something vague and uncertain into something productive and goal-oriented. Effort is valuable, but it's when you can see the results of that effort that you turn action into tangible progress.

7. Encourages Perseverance

Measuring progress isn't just about the good moments—it's about seeing your journey in its entirety. When you track your progress, you recognize both your successes and the challenges you've overcome. This holistic view of your journey encourages perseverance. You begin to understand that growth is a process, not an event. The setbacks and struggles become part of the progress, not evidence of failure. When you measure, you see that even in difficult seasons, you are still moving forward.

8. Transforms Dreams into Reality

Ultimately, measuring your progress transforms dreams into reality. It takes what once seemed far away or impossible and breaks it down into achievable steps. With every measurement, you move closer to making your vision tangible. Big dreams are made of small, measured steps, and when you track your progress, you witness the gradual unfolding of your goals. This practice brings your future into the present, helping you realize that your dream is not only possible but already in motion.

9. Builds Confidence and Momentum

As you measure your progress, you build confidence. There is power in seeing tangible evidence of your growth. Knowing that you are making real strides toward your goals reinforces your belief in your own abilities. Each step forward builds momentum, and as you gather that momentum, your capacity to achieve expands. Measuring progress is like fuel for your confidence, propelling you with the assurance that you are capable of greatness.

10. Aligning with Purpose

Measuring your progress also keeps you aligned with your purpose. It's a way of ensuring that the actions you take are consistent with the person you're becoming. As you measure, you reflect on whether your efforts are leading you toward the fulfillment of your God-given purpose. This alignment is crucial for making progress that is not only successful but also meaningful. Progress without purpose is empty, but when you align your progress with your purpose, every step takes on deeper significance.

Measuring your progress is about more than simply tracking accomplishments; it's about cultivating awareness, celebrating your growth, and staying aligned with your purpose. When you measure, you gain clarity, motivation, and the insight needed to keep moving forward. It's a practice that turns vague aspirations into concrete achievements and ensures that every effort you make is moving you closer to the life you were created to live.

Progress doesn't happen by accident—it's the result of intentional, measured steps that bring you closer to your vision. Each measurement is a milestone, a reflection of how far you've come, and a signpost directing you toward what's next.

CHAPTER 7

KINGDOM IDENTITY

…' But the people that do know their God shall be strong,
and do exploits.' Daniel 11:32

Progress is the culture of Zion and the identifying factor of a child of God. It is abnormal to be comfortable in the same position for an unhealthy period of time. God is committed to our progress, so we should be too (Proverbs 4:18). You are therefore not permitted to go around in circles.

Redundancy and stagnation are anti-God. They keep you on one spot and sap you of the much-needed strength for your journey. We will discover how our kingdom identity is defined by the progress we make on a daily basis. God's measuring standard is not how far we have come but how faithful we are to the call to make progress.

Progress: Our Kingdom Identity
God has great plans of progress for you and generations after you. The lives of our covenant fathers proved this. Abraham was great, Isaac was very great, and Jacob was exceedingly great.

A life void of progress is a burden. You are a child of God, and your salvation package includes progress. God thoughtfully built this in so that your pilgrimage on earth will be a glorious one. He will see to it that the devil does not put you to shame.

Whatever endeavor you are on, that does not indicate any sign of progress should be reevaluated. Either you are in the wrong space, not doing the right thing, or not doing it right.

The path of the just shines more and more until the appearing of Jesus. Psalm 75:6-7 clearly tells us that God is the judge, and it is he who promotes. A life devoid of promotion and increase is a disgrace to Zion. Let us take a look at Proverbs 22:29.

> *"29"*Seest thou a man diligent in his business? he
> shall stand before kings; he shall not stand
> before mean men.

God wants to bless whatever you have in your hand until you become exceedingly great. You are in a relationship with a great God who has a great destiny in store for you. Don't settle for less!

Small Beginnings: The Kingdom Way
Your unfavorable reality today is immaterial as long as you are in a covenant relationship with God. Greatness is your lot! Job mentioned this in Job 8:6-7.

> *"6*If thou wert pure and upright; surely now he
> would awake for thee, and make the habitation
> of thy righteousness prosperous. *7*Though thy
> beginning was small, yet thy latter end should
> greatly increase.

Although our covenant does not forbid small beginnings, it will be a sin against your destiny to remain on a small estate. Covenant is opposed to mediocrity, so don't harbor it. In the beginning, God created two people – male and female (Genesis 1:27). Today, there are over 8 billion people in the world.

The Bible is replete with scriptures that attest to the fact that God loves to do business with people of low estate and take them to higher levels of glory (Proverbs 13:11, Ecclesiastes 3:11, and Isaiah 60:22).

Inexhaustible Blessings: Kingdom Alignment Indicator

No matter how comfortable or otherwise you are right now, you need to realize that there are more blessings apportioned for you in the heavenly places (Ephesians1:3).

It is unimaginable the blessings that God wants to bestow upon His children in these last days. It is on planet Earth that we need them to showcase us and distinguish us from the rest of the world. Heaven has no need. The streets are paved with gold (Revelation 21:21). Go after what redemption has offered you so that you won't lose out. Your father is the almighty God, and you are not supposed to live like a pauper. The house of Jacob (you) has not been called to seek Him in vain.

> [19]I have not spoken in secret, in a dark place of
> the earth: I said not unto the seed of Jacob, Seek
> ye me in vain: I the LORD speak righteousness,
> I declare things that are right.

Isaiah 45:19

The subject of progress does not cover only material blessings. It covers every good thing that life has to offer.

God wants your progress to be visible so that unbelievers will be attracted to Him. God is not into secret dealings. He will set a table for you in the presence of your adversaries and make a big show of His glory upon your life.

Wilderness Journey: Experiencing Kingdom Alignment

As long as you are sure of God's leading, your wilderness experience is a sign of progress. It will turn out for your good. Progress is an advancement in the good things of life. It is going forward in the counsel of God.

For instance, God instructed the Israelites to leave Egypt for Canaan, to pass through the desert with its extreme temperature fluctuations. God needed them to be strengthened through these unfavorable circumstances so that they could develop the capacity to face the giants in Canaan. As far as God was concerned, they were progressing through the wilderness experience.

God's definition of progress is different from man's. For instance, in the kingdom of God, materialism is not always a sign of progress. The process matters to God. Ultimately, he measures our progress by our closeness to Him and His Son, Jesus Christ.

Keys to Kingdom Identity

Deep in our souls, we all long to have an identity. Kingdom identity is different from worldly identity. Our identity transcends this temporal world. As spiritual beings navigating a physical realm, we often find ourselves grappling with questions of who we are and where we belong. The Bible offers profound insights into our true identity as heirs of the kingdom of God. Embarking on this journey, we uncover seven keys that unlock the essence of our kingdom identity, guiding us towards a life of spiritual fulfillment and divine purpose.

Knowing God as Father

The foundational key to understanding our identity in the kingdom lies in recognizing God as our loving father. Throughout scripture, God reveals Himself as a tender and compassionate father who cares deeply for His children. In the parable of the Prodigal Son (Luke 15:11-32), Jesus vividly illustrates the father's heart of unconditional love and forgiveness. No matter how far we stray, God eagerly awaits our return, ready to embrace us with open arms.

Embracing Sonship through Christ

Our identity as sons and daughters of God is made possible through the sacrificial death and resurrection of Jesus Christ. Through His blood, we are cleansed from sin and adopted into God's family (Ephesians 1:5). This profound act of grace not only redeems us from bondage but also grants us the privilege of inheritance as co-heirs with Christ (Romans 8:17). By embracing our sonship in Christ, we inherit the riches of God's kingdom and enjoy intimate communion with our heavenly father.

Renewing the mind with truth

The process of renewing our minds with kingdom truths is an ongoing journey of spiritual growth and transformation. As the apostle Paul admonishes in Romans 12:2, we are called to resist conformity to the world's patterns and instead allow God's Word to shape our thoughts and beliefs. Through meditation, study, and application of Scripture, we dismantle the lies of the enemy and embrace the truth of God's word. The Holy Spirit plays a vital role in this process, illuminating scripture and empowering us to live in accordance with kingdom principles.

Walking in authority and power

As citizens of God's Kingdom, we are endowed with spiritual authority and power to combat the forces of darkness and advance God's purposes on earth. Jesus conferred this authority upon His disciples, empowering them to heal the sick, cast out demons, and proclaim the gospel (Matthew 10:1; Mark 16:17-18). Through prayer, faith, and obedience to God's Word, we exercise our authority as ambassadors of Christ, demonstrating the reality of His kingdom through signs and wonders.

Cultivating a kingdom mindset

A kingdom mindset redirects our focus from temporal concerns to eternal realities, prioritizing God's kingdom above all else. Jesus exhorts us to seek first the Kingdom of God and His righteousness, promising that all our needs will be provided (Matthew 6:33). By aligning our thoughts and desires with God's kingdom agenda, we transcend the pursuit of earthly success and significance. Instead, we invest our time, talents, and resources in building God's kingdom and advancing His purposes on earth.

Walking in holiness and righteousness

Holiness and righteousness are essential attributes of our kingdom identity, reflecting the character of our Heavenly Father. As Peter writes, we are called to be holy in all our conduct, imitating the one who called us (1 Peter 1:15-16). Through the power of the Holy Spirit, we are sanctified and empowered to live lives that are pleasing to God. Holiness involves both a separation from sin and a consecration to God's purposes as we surrender our will to His leading.

Fulfilling our kingdom assignment

Each of us is uniquely called and commissioned to fulfill a specific kingdom assignment, ordained by God before the foundation of the world. Just as God appointed Moses to deliver the Israelites from bondage and Paul to preach the gospel to the Gentiles, He has a divine purpose for each of us (Exodus 3:10; Acts 9:15). Discovering and embracing our kingdom assignment requires seeking God's guidance through prayer, seeking wise counsel, and stepping out in faith. As we align our lives with God's purposes, we experience a sense of fulfillment and satisfaction that transcends earthly achievements.

Our kingdom identity is rooted in our relationship with God as our loving father, established through the redemptive work of Jesus Christ, and empowered by the Holy Spirit. By renewing our minds with kingdom truths, walking in authority and power, cultivating a kingdom mindset, pursuing holiness and righteousness, and fulfilling our kingdom assignment, we embrace the fullness of who God created us to be.

As citizens of God's kingdom, we are called to live lives that reflect His glory, proclaim His truth, and advance His kingdom on earth. May we embrace these seven keys to kingdom identity and walk in the abundant life that God has prepared for us.

CHAPTER 8

THERE IS HOPE FOR YOU!

If the subject of this discussion makes you feel like an outcaste, there is hope for you! No matter the state you are in, there is hope for you! Perhaps you see a bleak future ahead of you. You are not permitted to give up on yourself because God has confidence in you. He invested so much in you, and He can beat His chest with the materials he configured you with (Psalm 139:14). You are a wonder on two legs!

Prophetic Declaration: No Shame in Hope
Now, you could be dwelling in the mud. The sky looks so dark that your world is filled with darkness. There is hope for you! In your marriage, the fruit of the womb could be a clog in the wheel of your progress. There is hope for you! Perhaps, as a student, failure has been your only companion. There is hope for you! You have labored tirelessly, and another person has come to reap your rewards. Take heart; there is hope for you!

> "⁷for there is hope for a tree if It is cut down, that it will sprout again. ⁸And that its tender shoots will not cease though its stump may die in the ground, ⁹yet at the scent of water it will bud and bring forth branches like a plant.
>
> Job 14:7- 9

There is hope for you because you are joined to a living God. It is not over with you yet! God has come with a new beginning for you. Let all men and the devil be liars, but God alone be true. The promises of God for your life can never fail.

Embrace the light you are contacting now, because darkness will surrender to light any day. The former is simply unable to comprehend the latter! This book has come your way to enhance the recovery of your inheritance in Christ Jesus.

Only water can turn a desert into a garden. The word of God is the water of life (Ephesians 5:26). The revelation of the word of God that this book brings will cause a revolution in your life. I can see your desert turning to the garden of Eden in Jesus' precious name.

Don't stop believing in the glorious future God has for you. What you don't believe, you cannot become. In the final analysis, it is the one who believes he can that does.

> "⁵Now hope does not disappoint, because the
> love of God has been poured out in our hearts by
> the Holy Spirit who was given to us.
> Romans 5:5

The knowledge of your inheritance is paramount to your recovery. Since progress is the will of God, if your life is devoid of it, you are permitted to react violently.

Prophetic Declaration: Move Forward with Hope
God's covenant forbids repeating the same class over and over again. That means repeatedly going over the same

issues, year in and year out. You have not failed until you stop trying, so get up! Whatever you don't permit will not happen. You should not be a description of failure. Why should you be the least in your class? Until you react against the reproach of failure, you can never become the epitome of success.

Redundancy is a trick of the devil to chip away at your destiny. You must spiritually resist anyone who stands against you receiving the rewards of your labor. God does not want you to labor in vain. You are not to labor for an unbeliever to consume. Rather, the reverse should be the case (Isaiah 49:23). God wants the labor of your hands to prosper, so that His glory can be evident in your life.

God wants your business to be profitable. He wants you to progress so that you can expand the place of your dwelling. He wants you to diversify your business interests so that your financial status can change. You should, in return, promote his kingdom.

As a minister of the gospel, God wants you to go forward. He wants that church to grow from ten to a hundred and from hundreds to thousands. He wants that evangelical work to progress from hamlets to villages, villages to cities, and countries to continents.

Prophetic Declaration: There's Hope for Your Marriage
God's progress package covers your marriage. Your marriage, by reason of the covenant, is not permitted to suffer any form of miscarriage or loss. God's comfort is upon your family and right now! You will progress in that which you have laid your hands upon to do!

"¹Comfort ye, comfort ye my people, saith your
God. ²Speak ye comfortably to Jerusalem, and
cry unto her, that her warfare is accomplished,
that her iniquity is pardoned: for she hath
received of the LORD'S hand double for all her
sins.

Isaiah 40:1-2

I declare war against any form of stagnation in your marriage
and family. The mercy of God is now on your coast; embrace
it!

Prophetic Declaration: My Walk with God
Your Christian journey will from today be characterized by
progress! God wants you to move forward, no matter the
opposition around you. He does not want you to backslide.
Rather, He wants you to grow in faith. You are to grow from
childhood to sonship, from a baby to a boy, and finally, a
man, so that your enthronement can be a reality.
Luke warmness does not portray progress, so cast it away!
Progress in the kingdom can be reached only by the
application of the force of faith.

The light you need to shatter every form of darkness in your
life has come. Embrace it! Knowledge is power, and
ignorance is a lack of knowledge or understanding. I see you
choosing knowledge!

Prophetic Declaration: I am not Ignorant
A man embarked on a 3-week-long journey by sea. At meal
times, everyone had to go to the canteen to pick up their
food. The man refused because he did not have enough

money on him. For two weeks, he nibbled on the biscuits he brought along with him.

After a while, someone took note of him and asked why he had not visited the canteen all along. The ignorant man gave a lack of money as an excuse. The kind fellow was quick to inform him that the ticket purchased for the journey covered food and other necessities. Oh, how bad the man felt! He had been suffering needlessly. This story explains the situation of many Christians. Your suffering has ended in the mighty name of Jesus!

Jesus Christ has paid for everything that will make your journey on earth colorful. You are destined for progress! You are a candidate for glory! Progress is part of your salvation package. It is an affliction of ignorance for a believer to carry the cross of regression. 2 Corinthians 5:21 says:

> "²¹For he hath made him [Jesus] to be sin for us,
> who knew no sin; that we might be made the
> righteousness of God in him.

God needs you to know your place in His kingdom. You are a kingdom financial star, so don't give in to Satan. We need money to spread the gospel around the world. You are a kingdom financier! You hold the key, so use it! Don't just stand by the wells of salvation; draw progress out so that your life can have meaning.

Prophetic Declaration: I make an Impact
You were created to demonstrate mental prowess. You will increase in knowledge and become an embodiment of wisdom! The Holy Spirit in you will strengthen you! God

wants you to be a star in your discipline. As a student, you should be exemplary in all you do.

Some Christian professionals constructed the Faith Tabernacle, Nigeria, the largest church auditorium in Nigeria. In 1999, Ike Chukwuneke, a structural engineer won the *Nigerian Society of Engineers (NSE) Engineer of the Year* award for the design of the edifice. That is distinction! That is what God wants for all His saints in their various life endeavors.

We are living in difficult times when progress is alien to many. This is especially true in developing countries, where it is common to find people moving around in circles trying to eke out a living. Today, I declare that your impact will be felt! You will not pass through this world for the sake of passing. Your voice will be heard!

Prophetic Declaration! My Help comes from God!
Isaac's progress, which was a point of envy to the government of the day, was the blessing of God. Isaac, like David, quoted below, called upon God for help.

> "[1]I will lift up mine eyes unto the hills, from
> whence cometh my help. [2]My help cometh from
> the LORD, which made heaven and earth.
>
> Psalm 121: 1-2.

Your progress is assured in the face of difficulties. The church of God, in the last days, will be the envy of the world.

(Isaiah 2:1-4). Many are claiming their covenant blessings already. Claim yours in Jesus' name!

The world may be teetering on the brink of a bad situation, with inflation staring many countries in the face. Many companies have gone bankrupt, and the effects of global warming and climate change are undeniable. These facts, notwithstanding, your case is different! Your identification with Christ makes the difference. God is very keen to show you off to the world.

We are in the last days, and God is winding up his program on earth that has lasted 1999 years and some fractions of months.

This generation has witnessed many of the signs of the end of the age, as detailed in Matthew 24. It is a great privilege to be around to witness such monumental times in the history of man.

So, arise and take your place! Time is running out. You are the light of the world and the salt of the earth (Mathew 5:13-16). Do not refuse to shine and lose your preservative power. You will give an account of the grace of God in your life. Don't sell out to the devil, like Esau did.

Prophetic Declaration: My Attitude Will Change
It is your attitude that will cause you to lay hold on hope. It will determine your altitude. Change it for the better! You are not supposed to have on earth whatever heaven does not have in stock. If you have stolen or illegal materials in your possession, you will be accused of stealing. Stagnancy is stolen property. Throw it away! It will find its way to where

it belongs – hell! Only then, can you take your place as a king on Earth.

The suffering of man is at an all-time high. People are groping around in the dark, looking for a way out. Will you be a light to the world?

> "¹⁴Ye are the light of the world. A city that is set on an hill cannot be hid. ¹⁵Neither do men light a candle, and put it under a bushel, but on a candlestick; and it giveth light unto all that are in the house. ¹⁶ Let your light so shine before men, that they may see your good works, and glorify your Father which is in heaven.
>
> Mathew 5:14 -16

Jesus is the one to approach when problems come. He alone holds the solution to all problems in life. Look up to Him in faith, and the light of His countenance will shine upon you. Your connection with Jesus makes you a candidate for His mercy.

No one ever came to Jesus and went back disappointed. If you do not approach Him with your problem, you will not find a lasting solution. The solution lies with Him. In Him we live, move, and have our being.

When storms of life assail you, separate yourself from the multitude to the prince of solution. You will find engaging in spiritual exercises - meditation on the word of God, prayers, and reading the Bible, very helpful at times like these (Proverbs 18:1). This is the way to secure your breakthrough.

Distraction: A Sign of Confusion

In Mark 8:22-25, quoted earlier, Jesus had to take the blind man out of his busy environment in order to give him the help he desired. The world is in a fast lane, and the frenzy can be overwhelming. Distractions pull us in different directions. The progressive candidate must know how to navigate his way.

When you are able to tackle the distractions in your life, you will be able to receive help from God. You will be able to look up to Him. Help from God comes from looking up first, not down, backwards, or around (Psalm 121) The blind man did not know how to look up until he was separated from the multitude.

When people have problems, they naturally look down or around for help. This is symbolic of blindness. It is natural to look around or downward when in need. Looking downward is an emblem of frustration and disappointment, while looking around is seeking help from men. Woe to him who puts his trust in man, says the Lord. Your problems have persisted because your focus is on men. Take a look at the very sobering scripture below:

> "[5]Thus saith the LORD; Cursed be the man that trusteth in man, and maketh flesh his arm, and whose heart departeth from the LORD." [6]For he shall be like the heath in the desert, and shall not see when good cometh; but shall inhabit the parched places in the wilderness, in a salt land and not inhabited."

> Jeremiah 17: 5-6.

The two 'looks' mentioned above show that you are focusing on your problems and not on God. What gets your attention is an indication of what you place a premium on.

Putting your trust in a man can be misleading. Over and above that, they are likely to mock you. Until you learn to put your trust in God by looking up, you will continually make bad decisions and end up hurting yourself and others.

Change of Focus: A Hope Enhancer
At a time in Abram's life, he took solace in Lot, his nephew, because he did not have a child of his own. God did not appear to him until he had separated from Lot. God is waiting for you too to take your eyes off men so that His help can flow towards you. Stop waiting on men! Start waiting on God! Those who wait upon the Lord will never see shame.

If God could ask Abram to change his focus to him, he would not say less to you (Genesis 13:14). Until you know how to lift up your eyes to God, you will never enjoy his lifting. Your inheritance in Christ is waiting for you to change your gaze. You will never receive it otherwise. It is possible to be by the riverside and yet die of thirst. From now on, anytime you have a need, talk to God first. Don't go around seeking help. Let God meet your needs anyhow He deems fit.

Hagar, Sarah's maid, felt the end had come to her son, Ishmael. His father, Abraham, had sent her and her son away at the request of Sarah. Right there, in her down moment, God reached out to her. God responded to the voice of the boy (Genesis 21:14 – 19).

Jesus, in His earthly ministry, was faced with a challenge at the death of Lazarus. He had to look up to heaven for help. Even though he was the anointed one, he couldn't do anything without a connection with heaven. (John 1:41).

We are all at the mercy of God. David, in Psalm 121:1, declared that help came from God.

The Apostle Paul declared that the help of God was his trade secret (Acts 26:22). It is the help of God that brings about progress. You cannot be helped by God and be stranded. Wherever God is, good things happen. The emblem of God over your destiny is perfection. He will complete whatever He has started in your life (James 1:17). You are His product, and every product will show the excellency of the manufacturer.

Some situations, like the one cited below, will require the additional touch of Jesus:

> "22 And he cometh to Bethsaida; and they bring a
> blind man unto him, and besought him to touch
> him. 23 And he took the blind man by the hand,
> and led him out of the town; and when he had
> spit on his eyes, and put his hands upon him, he
> asked him if he saw ought. 24 And he looked up,
> and said, I see men as trees, walking. 25 After
> that he put his hands again upon his eyes, and
> made him look up: and he was restored, and saw
> every man clearly.
>
> Mark 8:22-25

This blind man, after the anointed touch of Jesus, could only see men like trees, walking. They looked like moving trees to him. He was close to his miracle, but he needed a second touch. Jesus gave it to him.

Whatever God will not perfect, He will not start. As a minister of the gospel, don't give up. Continue to walk in faith, and you will reap a harvest of souls for the kingdom of God. Surely, the work of God will prosper in your hands. Look up to God for that extra touch that will stamp a seal of perfection over the work of your hands.

The blind man looked again, and his eye sight was restored. As you do the same, yours will be too. Help is always available for you in the heavenly places. For a long time now, you have been looking in the wrong places. You have not been looking up to God. It is no wonder your situation has remained stubborn, refusing to let you go. As a result, people have called you names like beggar, borrower, barren, destitute, etc.

When you begin to look to heaven, God will give you a new name. You will believe the verdict of God over that of man. Your heavenly father calls you blessed! Stop looking downward, because your frustration is ending now! Your depression is giving way to joy! Elevator lights need to be switched on for the elevator to take you up. Your light is on! Your lift is coming! Receive it in the mighty name of Jesus!

CHAPTER 9

THE ENEMY OF PROGRESS

**When Sanballat the Horonite and Tobiah the
Ammonite official heard of it, they were
deeply disturbed that a man had come to
seek the well-being of the children of Israel.
Nehemiah 2:10**

The devil is the enemy of progress. He celebrates stagnation and lack of progress in the lives of people, especially the people of God. His every action is geared towards the destruction of man (John10:10). Sometimes, he causes men to move around in circles to deceive them into believing that they are making progress. At other times, he may cause man to actually experience progress. You must understand that he has the power to offer men a good life. Not all good things are blessings from God, though. This is evidenced by the narrative of the temptation of Jesus in Matthew 4:1-11.

Hell Fire: The Deceiver's Ultimate Goal
The ultimate goal of the devil is to take the soul of man to hell (John 10:10). He is very crafty and will give nothing for nothing. Does anyone keep their money in the bank without the plan of withdrawing it someday? Find below an example of the devil's business model.

"[11]And the merchants of the earth shall weep and
mourn over her; for no man buyeth their

merchandise any more: [12] The merchandise of
gold, and silver, and precious stones, and of
pearls, and fine linen, and purple, and silk, and
scarlet, and all thyine wood, and all manner
vessels of ivory, and all manner vessels of most
precious wood, and of brass, and iron, and
marble,[13]And cinnamon, and odours, and
ointments, and frankincense, and wine, and oil,
and fine flour, and wheat, and beasts, and sheep,
and horses, and chariots, and slaves, and souls of
men.

Revelation 18:12-13

The souls of men listed as the last item are indicative of how much value the devil places on them. They mean more to him than the aforementioned items. Ultimately, man is his target. He wants to destroy him.

The Devil: Our Enemy
The devil is a trickster. He takes advantage of people because he knows that the desire of every reasonable human being is progress. Many, because of dissatisfaction with their lives, have fallen prey to his tactics. How so? They join the occult, visit herbalists, do shady business deals, and get involved in ritualistic activities.

[27]Nor give place to the devil"

Ephesians 4 :27

The soul of man is extremely precious. So much so that gaining the whole world cannot be compared to the colossal loss of a soul (Mark 8:36) The devil offers man the world to deceive and lead him into calamity. You should stand against his schemes and tactics.

Mind Games: The Devil's Tools for Bondage
Another way the devil impedes the progress of man is by attacking his emotions. That is why we are warned in the scripture above to give no place to him. When you give the devil an inch, he goes a mile. He afflicts Christians with anger, envy, bitterness, jealousy, etc. These negative feelings will hold you down. They constitute weights that will not allow you to make progress. They are also entry points for demonic possession and oppression. The correct application of the word of God and effectual and fervent prayers will break us free from the bondage of the devil (John 8:32; James 5:16).

Once you have secured your freedom in Christ, you should maintain it by constant study of God's word, prayers, and fellowship with the Children of God. The devil always seeks to rebind careless Christians (Matthew 12:43-45).

Resisting Satan: My Choice
Satan is a defeated foe. He knows he is doomed and wants to drag people to hell with him. He takes advantage of people's ignorance to prey on them. You are no longer under his control. You are no longer a victim, so resist him! (James 4:7). The devil will not let you go without a fight. He will relentlessly pursue you, with the aim of inflicting destruction on your soul.

Life is a matter of choice. You are a product of the decisions you make. It is in your power to choose what you want for yourself. From today on, make up your mind to turn your back on the devil.

> "¹⁷That made the world as a wilderness, and
> destroyed the cities thereof; that opened not the
> house of his prisoners?

> Isaiah 14:17

If ignorance leads people into the captivity of Satan, then knowledge is the only way to escape. As light has mastery over darkness, the light you are contacting now will establish your liberty (John 8:32). You are a captain in the kingdom of God; don't remain a captive of Satan's kingdom.

The world will have no choice but to acknowledge the supremacy of the church of the living God. Hear what God is saying in Isaiah 2:1–3:

> "¹The word that Isaiah the son of Amoz saw
> concerning Judah and Jerusalem. ²And it shall
> come to pass in the last days, that the mountain
> of the Lord's house shall be established in the
> top of the mountains, And shall be exalted above
> the hills; And nations shall flow unto it.³ And
> many people shall go and say, Come ye, and let
> us go up to the mountain of the Lord, To the
> house of the God of Jacob; And he will teach us
> of his ways, And we will walk in his paths: For
> out of Zion shall go forth the law, And the word
> of the Lord from Jerusalem.

Don't give in to Satan. This is the time of the church! This is your time!

Change of Mind Set: My Choice
Think right, because your thoughts will become your reality. Meditate on the word of God and the glorious future of the church of the living God. One of our great minds said, "If thoughts indeed become things, it is to our advantage to think good thoughts." Stop magnifying the devil by allowing him to infiltrate your thoughts."

Sin is the devil's trap. Don't fall into it! When you live in sin, you take yourself out of the boundaries of where God's love can reach and bless you (Jude1:21).

> [21]"Keep yourselves in the love of God, looking for the mercy of our Lord Jesus Christ unto eternal life."

Knowledge guarantees recovery. The difference between the winner and the loser, the rich and the poor, the fearful and the bold, the oppressed and the free, is knowledge. It has always been the distinguishing factor.

Guarding my Heart: My Choice
Man has a soul, lives in a body, and communicates with God through His regenerated spirit (1 Thessalonians 5:23). Your body is your connection to the natural realm; it is your earth suit. Your soul is the realm of decision where you have your mind, will, and emotions; it is the seat of your intellect. It is the neutral ground between your body and spirit. The soul is eternal. It is either redeemed (3 John 1:2) or unredeemed (Proverbs 21:10). Your spirit is your connection to God. It is the innermost part of who you are and the center of your

identity. It is through your spirit that you fellowship with God (1 Corinthians 2:10-12).

The devil's strategy is to attack your soul, which is a combination of your heart and mind. In effect, he goes for your heart and your mind. No wonder we are soberly charged in Proverbs 4:23 (quoted below) to guard our hearts with all diligence. If you don't, you will lose it. The devil enjoys playing mind games with people. He steals their peace and messes them up emotionally by endlessly feeding them lies.

> "23Keep your heart with all diligent for out of it
> springs the issue of life.

When the devil is able to penetrate your soul, he can keep you grounded and stagnated. Let your heart be saturated with the word of God. He will lift you up and cause you to soar like the eagle (Isaiah 40:31).

You are Overdue for a Change

Change is inevitable, and you must embrace it. God desires your progress because it brings glory to His name (Proverbs 4:18-22) Whatever you are involved in as a child of God should prosper because Jesus is in the boat of your life.

> "38And he was in the hinder part of the ship,
> asleep on a pillow: and they awake him, and say
> unto him, Master, carest thou not that we perish?
> 39 And he arose, and rebuked the wind, and said
> unto the sea, Peace, be still. And the wind
> ceased, and there was a great calm. 40 And he

said unto them, why are ye so fearful? how is it
that ye have no faith? [41] And they feared
exceedingly, and said one to another, what
manner of man is this, that even the wind and
the sea obey him?

Mark 4: 38 – 41

Jesus' presence in your life brings an end to stagnancy and redundancy in your life. It is the dawn of a new day for you! Beautiful days lie ahead of you! Receive it in Jesus' name! God has no glory in your stagnation. He is telling you to cross over. When you refuse to, you will be crushed by the problems of life. You need to break forth into a new phase of your life. You have remained in the same spot long enough.

The other side promises fruitfulness, accomplishments, progress, etc. If these were not so, God would never have invited you over. If He has said it, then it will come to pass.

If God cannot convince you, Satan will confuse you. There is no middle ground. You must take a stand. I see you standing on the word of God. Congratulations! I see you progressing in all areas of your life!

People: Assets or Liabilities

As you journey through life, you will discover that people can either be assets or liabilities. They could be a plus or a barrier to your progress. Seasons of life are indicated by the entry and exit of people into and out of our lives. You need to leave some people behind if you want to progress in life. If you refuse to, they could detract you from pursuing your purpose. The

84

average man is resistant to change – for himself and others. Because he resents the fact that you want to move ahead, he may try to stop you by intimidating you and belittling your efforts. See this for what it is and move on determinedly.

My entrance into full-time ministry met with stiff opposition from people. Some believed in my call but felt I needed to exercise patience. Others advised that I pursue it on a part-time basis. Some did not even believe in it at all. In fact, there were some people I chose not to inform at all because I knew the devil would attack my soul through them. When God has spoken, no man's vote is required for the attainment of your destiny.

By all means, avoid the philosophies of men. Don't go by the traditions of men, or else you will miss the additions of heaven over your life. People will try to convince you that you are making the wrong decision. All these are gimmicks of Satan to distract and stagnate you.

Your dream of progress is a threat to him. No matter his gimmicks and tactics, don't give up. When you are challenged, don't doubt the word of God because He will not change His mind. Rest assured that His presence is always with you.

"[1]But now thus saith the LORD that created thee,
O Jacob, and he that formed thee, O Israel, Fear
not: for I have redeemed thee, I have called thee
by thy name; thou art mine.[2]When thou passest
through the waters, I will be with thee; and
through the rivers, they shall not overflow thee:
when thou walkest through the fire, thou shalt
not be burned; neither shall the flame kindle
upon thee.

Isaiah 43 :1-2

Jesus' presence in the ship with his disciples did not stop a storm from rising. Something will always rise against you. You will always need to stand your ground against the devil; otherwise, progress will not be your reality.

Rebuke the Wind: Breaking into Progress

Many people lack the spiritual skills to address the winds of opposition blowing against them. Although they worked so hard to build thriving careers, their personal lives are in shambles. It has not occurred to them that success principles will not keep the devil at bay.

The disciples knew how to call on Jesus in the face of their predicament. A man in a pit needs help to come out. Your helper is waiting, but you need to call on him to get help. If you want to fulfill your destiny, you must call for help.

If you wait for Jesus to rebuke the wind for you, you will wait forever. Arise, because you have what it takes to do so. The authority conferred on Jesus by God is yours as well (John 20:21).

Leave the waves and focus on the wind. If you will be victorious in life battles, you need to address the problem from the root. When the wind is addressed, in a matter of time, the waves will cease to form. Take charge so that, like Jesus, the winds and waves will obey you (Mathew 8:27).

You are not expected to live like a wanderer. The wonders of God should be evident in all your endeavors.

Let us see other means that Satan may employ to derail your progress.

Science and Religion: Their Interconnectedness

Science and religion are interrelated. They both seek to understand the universe, how it works, and our place in it. According to Albert Einstein, "Science without religion is lame; religion without science is blind." The latter, according to the Oxford dictionary, is the systematic study of the structure and behavior of the physical and natural world through observation, experimentation, and the testing of theories against the evidence obtained. The latter, according to the same source, defines religion as the belief in and worship of a superhuman power or powers, especially of God or gods.

That being said, science should be jettisoned when it contravenes the authority of God's word.

> "[20]O Timothy, keep that which is committed to
> thy trust, avoiding profane and vain babblings,
> and oppositions of science falsely so called: [21]
> Which some professing have erred concerning
> the faith. Grace be with thee. Amen.
>
> 1 Timothy 6:20-21

Economists, because they can help investors understand the workings of natural policy and events on business conditions, may discourage investments at particular times. In periods of famine, popular opinion may favor relocation to more prosperous locations.

We know from the word of God in Genesis 26 that God is to be believed over all else. Isaac sowed in the thick of a famine and, in that same year, reaped a hundred-fold harvest. Abraham was 100 years old when Sarah gave birth to Isaac. She was 90 years old.

Talk about putting the laws of menopause to shame! May your life receive the energy, force, and power of the Holy Ghost in the mighty name of Jesus.

Government and Politics: Our Reality

Whether we like it or not, our lives are influenced by the policies enacted by the government (1Timothy 2:1-2). The worldwide COVID-19 lockdowns showed us how our lives are affected by government policies. When the government takes a stand, responsible Christians, in accordance with God's word in Mark 12:17, comply. Christians should be law abiding citizens.

However, a wrong policy by the government could make life difficult for you and derail the attainment of your purpose. This underscores the need for us to regularly pray for our leaders.

> "[15]And when money failed in the land of Egypt, and in the land of Canaan, all the Egyptians

came unto Joseph, and said, Give us bread: for
why should we die in thy presence? for the
money faileth.

Genesis 47:15

Occurrences like wars, epidemics, famine, death, etc. are the avenues through which our progress could be hampered. With God on your side, you have what it takes to move your life forward. Do not allow your life circumstances to hold you down.

You have the authority to subdue, dominate, and pull down every work of Satan. Stop that family curse from alighting! Come against the spirit of death that is hovering over you or your family members! Satan will capitalize on these situations to confine you.

CHAPTER 10

BARRIERS TO PROGRESS

"¹Now Jericho was straitly shut up because of
the children of Israel: none went out, and none
came in.

Joshua 6:1

The devil will do everything he can to erect barriers in the way of Christians to withhold them from possessing their inheritance. Barriers are synonymous with limitations, barricades, impossibilities, etc. When they are in place, progress is impossible. What believers need to do is pull down the walls of doubt, confinement, unbelief, fear, etc. The promises of God as contained in the Holy Bible are true.

The Traditions of Men
The life of a Christian should be one of receiving divine instructions. You have a problem if you cannot hear from heaven. Anytime a man's life is devoid of the voice of the Holy Spirit, his life will eventually be in crisis.

Sometimes, evil company debars you from receiving your blessings (Proverbs 13:20). You have to do away with some relationships. Take the time to commune with God, and He will instruct you. Your own 'Lot' could be the traditions of men.

If you want to abide by the traditions of men or family impositions, you will miss the tradition of heaven. Many Christians are unable to take a stand against the harmful and unscriptural cultural activities practiced in their homes and communities.

Stop it now, in the mighty name of Jesus! Turn your back on idol worship! Stop fetishism now!

Let's now take a look at the ways the enemy can forestall a Christian's progress when questions of sin have been answered.

The Trap of the Past

Every believer has a destiny of sustained glory in Christ Jesus (Romans 8:30). The traps of the past must be avoided if you will apprehend your destiny.

> "[50]And unto Joseph were born two sons before
> the years of famine came, which Asenath the
> daughter of Potipherah priest of On bare unto
> him. [51]And Joseph called the name of the
> firstborn Manasseh: For God, said he, hath made
> me forget all my toil, and all my father's house.
> [52]And the name of the second called he Ephraim:
> For God hath caused me to be fruitful in the land
> of my affliction.
>
> Genesis 41: 50-52

God is progressive, and he desires that his children be forward-looking in nature. This explains why men's eyes are in front and not at the back. Physically, looking back may result in a stumble or fall, but looking back spiritually can be life-threatening. Our life purpose is on the line when we fail to press forward (Philippians 3:13–14).

You must develop the emotional intelligence to manage the seasons of your life - your past, present, and future. The future becomes the present, and the present becomes the past. They are all interconnected.

We can draw lessons from the testimonies of people like Jephthah, who refused to allow his past to rob him of his present and future.

> "¹Now Jephthah the Gileadite was a mighty man
> of valour, and he was the son of an harlot: and
> Gilead begat Jephthah.
>
> Judges 11:1

Jephthah was an outcast and a rebel, and yet "the Spirit of the Lord came upon him." (Judges 11-12). Regardless of your upbringing, status, or place in life, God can still use you.

Satan is an accuser of the brethren, and he is relentless in his attacks (Revelation 12:10). He digs up our past and brings it before God. Fortunately, his accusations fall on deaf ears.

Push past your past into a glorious present and future. Until you let go of your past, like Joseph and Jephthah, your fruitfulness will not materialize.

"⁹And Jephthah said unto the elders of Gilead, If
ye bring me home again to fight against the
children of Ammon, and the LORD deliver them
before me, shall I be your head? ¹⁰And the elders
of Gilead said unto Jephthah, The LORD be
witness between us, if we do not so according to
thy words. ¹¹Then Jephthah went with the elders
of Gilead, and the people made him head and
captain over them: and Jephthah uttered all his
words before the LORD in Mizpeh.

Judges 11:9-11

God never consults your past to determine your future. Your
past is past, so let it go! Learn from it, but let it go. The past
is irreparable, but the present and future are not.

My New Life in Christ: Unwrapping my Destiny
Our lives can effectively be divided into two: the one outside
Christ and the new life in Christ Jesus. Our new life in Christ
dictates that we live by faith (Habakkuk 2:4) and not by
relying on observing the law. The failure to do all that is
written in the book of the law attracts a curse (Galatians
3:10). This is further explained in Deuteronomy 28:15.

"¹⁵But it shall come to pass, if thou wilt not
hearken unto the voice of the LORD thy God, to
observe to do all his commandments and his
statutes which I command thee this day; that all
these curses shall come upon thee, and overtake
thee:

By virtue of our relationship with Jesus Christ, we become new creations (2 Corinthians 5:17). The old Adam led us into the sin and slavery of Satan. The new Adam gave us liberty. Christ redeemed us from the curse of the law (Galatians 3:13-14). This extraordinary deed sets us free from the bondage of sin and the accusations of the devil (Galatians 3:13-14).

Two people cannot suffer for the same offense. Since Jesus Christ paid the price for your sin, why should you pay it again? Apprehend your blessings and walk in your liberty now!

Stop seeing yourself in the light of your past. Using the word of God, paint a picture of the glorious future that redemption has secured for you.

> "[12]For I will be merciful to their
> unrighteousness, and their sins and their
> iniquities will I remember no more.
>
> Hebrew 8:12

Don't allow the devil to capitalize on your ignorance. God has freed you, so you are free. Live in this reality! Redemption has given you a new record; therefore, you are qualified for Abrahamic blessings.

Stagnation: The Devil's Trap
The devil uses failure to cause stagnation in people's lives. The fact that you failed does not make you a failure. Failure is an event or occurrence in a person's life. You need not define yourself by occurrences that are fleeting. You are not

a failure until you admit that you are one. What people call you is immaterial. What you call yourself is what matters. What do you believe about yourself? Do you see yourself as able? Whose report do you believe? I hear you saying, "God's!"

You possess the power to create a new beginning when the devil strikes. If there is no seat at the table for you, bring yours along! You have a voice! So, use it! Don't sit around throwing a pity party.

We are slaves to what we are ignorant of. There is a wise solution to every problem, so seek knowledge. With it, you can disarm all the forces of wickedness arrayed against you. Isaac subdued all the devils around him. His success story is outlined in Genesis 26:18–22. The enemies rose up against him, but he refused to succumb to them. He didn't accept the suggestions of the opposition. Any past circumstance that does not positively influence your destiny should be discarded.

Release the people who hurt you in the past, so you can move forward. Although the herdsmen of Gerar filled Isaac's well up with earth, he didn't allow his heart to be filled with bitterness against them.

For every door the enemy closes in your life, God promises a replacement. While the devil can toil with your past, he has no access to your future. Your destiny is secured in Christ Jesus. Go and dig again, you will find water!

The devil also stagnates believers with their past successes. According to Jerry Rice, 'The enemy of the best is the good."

If you're always settling for what's good, you'll never get the best. You are not at the climax of God's blessings. In fact, there is no climax to His blessings. God is in the business of doing new things all the time. With Him, there is always a next level.

> "¹⁸Remember ye not the former things, neither consider the things of old. ¹⁹Behold, I will do a new thing; now it shall spring forth; shall ye not know it? I will even make a way in the wilderness, and rivers in the desert.

> Isaiah 43:18-19

Looking backward is a pacesetter for stagnation, while looking forward sets you up for success. No one who runs a race and keeps looking back will win the prize. Let the past go so that you can move forward.

The Trap of Idleness

> "¹²Then Isaac sowed in that land, and received in the same year an hundredfold: and the LORD blessed him.¹³And the man waxed great, and went forward, and grew until he became very great:

> Genesis 26:12-13

It is through work that God prospers man. It is the work of His hands that His power will rest on. A jobless man is not a candidate for God's prosperity. Zero multiplied by any number amounts to zero. In the same vein, whatever you add zero to amounts to the same number. What I am saying, in effect, is that God's blessings need a seed of labor to latch upon. It will not work otherwise. Had Isaac not sown in the land, he would not have reaped the hundredfold return.

Prayers, fasting, meditation, giving, and other spiritual activities are very useful to tackle stagnation and a lack of financial prosperity. However, they will never replace work. When you have nothing to do, you make it difficult for God to bless you. All our covenant fathers worked hard to qualify for God's blessings. Paul, our apostle of grace, prospered not only by grace, but also by hard work (Acts 20:34-35).

The dignity of labor dictates that no legitimate means of livelihood should be relegated or extolled over and above another. You should never be ashamed of your work. Rather, be ashamed of not doing anything. Wealth gained by vanity shall diminish. You will be unable to sustain any wealth you acquire without work.

Until you work, nothing works for you. The cheapest way to be ridiculed is to hang around men for survival. It is a shameful existence.

You should be well engaged in your family, church, and society. Idleness will take a toll on your mental health. Usually, it ultimately leads to hopelessness and depression (Proverb 6:10-11).

If you sleep more than is necessary, poverty will be your identity. Jesus, the author and finisher of our faith, was a hard worker. In John 9:4, he said he needed to do the works of God while it was day. Engage with the Holy Spirit and use your brain to work your way out of poverty.

If a man bears his yoke in his youth, his old age will not be cursed. Furthermore, God expects us to bear fruit in old age. Sow your seeds as a youth, and you will reap them in manifold returns many years later (Psalm 92:14). You can, through the avenue of work, work your way to the top. Only the diligent will dine with the noble men of the earth.

The Trap of Indolence

When a man is careless about the progress of the kingdom of God, he should not expect God to be committed to his affairs. When people take God's matters with levity, they pay for it. No matter how successful they become, they eventually lose out because God cannot be mocked. It is not unusual to find people spending so much time on their work at the detriment of God's own. This practice is unacceptable to God and has consequences. We should be spiritually intelligent enough to draw the balance between the two.

"3Then came the word of the LORD by Haggai
the prophet, saying, 4Is it time for you, O ye, to
dwell in your cieled houses, and this house lie
waste? 5Now therefore thus saith the LORD of
hosts; Consider your ways.6Ye have sown much,
and bring in little; ye eat, but ye have not
enough; ye drink, but ye are not filled with
drink; ye clothe you, but there is none warm;
and he that earneth wages earneth wages to put it
into a bag with holes. 7Thus saith the LORD of
hosts; Consider your ways.8Go up to the
mountain, and bring wood, and build the house;
and I will take pleasure in it, and I will be
glorified, saith the LORD.

Haggai 1:3-8.

We are admonished to seek the kingdom of God first, and all the blessings we earnestly desire will be granted to us (Matthew 6:33). Note the word 'first'. God still expects us to be committed to our secular work (Ephesians 6:5-9). The Kingdom of God is of utmost importance because it is through our right interactions with it that we gain eternal life.

If the devil blocks man's way, he calls on God. Who does he call upon when God resists him for his disobedience? You can secure God's support all the time by investing in His kingdom. His work should be food for you (John 4:34).

God has a place for you in His body, that of Christ. Arise, shine, and let no man take your crown. Fill a gap in the kingdom, and God will fill the gaps in your life.

More Barriers to Progress

In our journey through life, we encounter various obstacles that hinder our progress and growth. These barriers, whether internal or external, can impede our pursuit of success, fulfillment, and spiritual maturity.

However, armed with wisdom from the scriptures, we can overcome these challenges and move forward with confidence and purpose. Here, we see the seven common barriers to progress. We also draw inspiration from the timeless truths of the Bible to break down these obstacles.

Fear and anxiety

Fear and anxiety often paralyze us, preventing us from taking risks and pursuing our goals. Yet, the Bible repeatedly admonishes us not to fear but to trust in God's provision and protection (Isaiah 41:10). By placing our trust in God's unfailing love and sovereignty, we can overcome fear and step boldly into the future.

Doubt and uncertainty

Doubt and uncertainty can erode our confidence and undermine our ability to make decisions. However, the scriptures remind us of the importance of faith and trust in God's wisdom and guidance (James 1:6).

By cultivating a steadfast faith in God's promises and seeking His direction through prayer and meditation on His Word, we can overcome doubt and walk in confidence.

Self-Doubt and insecurity

Self-doubt and insecurity can sabotage our efforts and prevent us from realizing our full potential. Yet, the Bible affirms our worth and identity as beloved children of God (Psalm 139:14). By embracing our identity in Christ and recognizing our value as His precious creation, we can silence the voice of self-doubt and love and accept ourselves the way we are.

Procrastination and laziness

Procrastination and laziness rob us of productivity and hinder our progress towards our goals. However, the Bible exhorts us to be diligent and industrious in our pursuits (Proverbs 6:6-8). By cultivating a spirit of diligence and discipline, we can overcome procrastination and laziness and make steady progress towards our objectives.

Negative thinking

Negative thinking can undermine our confidence and efforts. The scriptures, in Philippians 4:8, remind us to guard our minds and focus on thoughts that are true, noble, right, pure, lovely, and admirable. By renewing our minds with the truth of God's Word and rejecting negative thought patterns, we can cultivate a positive mindset and overcome self-sabotaging behaviors. Thinking ill of people and harboring envious feelings are other ways we can destroy ourselves. You cannot make progress while you are trying to keep others down.

Resistance to change

Resistance to change can keep us stuck in unhealthy patterns and prevent us from growing. However, the Bible encourages us to embrace change as a necessary part of our journey towards spiritual maturity. By surrendering to God's transformative work in our lives and trusting in His faithfulness, we can embrace change as an opportunity for growth and progress (Romans 12:1-2).

Lack of faith in God's providence

Lack of faith in God's providence can hinder our progress and limit our potential. The Bible assures us of God's faithfulness and provision in every circumstance (Matthew 6:25-26). By placing our trust in God's unfailing love and provision, we can overcome anxiety and uncertainty and move forward with confidence and assurance.

CHAPTER 11

PROGRESS ENHANCERS

Progress, like every life activity, has its own pathway for attainment. Understanding the principles that underpin it is helpful to achieve it. A principle is a theorem or law that can be applied to different situations. This means that there are certain rules or codes of conduct that can be applied by different people at different times to make progress in their lives (Isaiah 28:10).

We should be intentional in our efforts to make progress. A lack of intentionality will slow us down and ultimately distract us from our goal.

Progress: A Covenant Issue
There are terms of engagement in any covenant. The Abrahamic Covenant is our guarantee of progress. While it cannot be contested, we have to play our part for us to be able to actualize it. The confirmation of the covenant is stated below.

"[9]Which covenant he made with Abraham, and his oath unto Isaac; [10]And confirmed the same unto Jacob for a law, and to Israel for an everlasting covenant:

Psalm 105:9-10.

Once man sets out to play his role, God is bound to play His part in the covenant. Abraham entered into the covenant by obeying God.

> "¹Now the LORD had said unto Abram, Get thee out of thy country, and from thy kindred, and from thy father's house, unto a land that I will shew thee: ²And I will make of thee a great nation, and I will bless thee, and make thy name great; and thou shalt be a blessing: ³And I will bless them that bless thee, and curse him that curseth thee: and in thee shall all families of the earth be blessed. ⁴So Abram departed, as the LORD had spoken unto him; and Lot went with him: and Abram was seventy and five years old when he departed out of Haran.
>
> Genesis 12:1-4

Until Abraham fulfilled his part, God never demonstrated His act. Obedience to the terms of God's covenant is what qualifies a man for His blessings. Your obedience to God commits Him to your affairs (Genesis 22:15-16).

God is a respecter of persons and also not a respecter of persons. This sounds contradictory, but that is simply how it is. He respects all who follow the terms of the covenant and will not prevent anyone from entering into the covenant with him. God demands obedience from us. This is the lesson we learn from the call of Abraham (Isaiah 51:2).

Let's take a look at some principles that enhance progress.

Believe in progress

You cannot become what you do not believe you can become. At the end of the day, you become what you believe. Your belief in progress is like signing an agreement with God that you deserve it (Proverbs 23:7). Your thought life will produce your success or failure. Believe in God's ability to move you forward. Don't look down on yourself. You are not a product of chance. Don't allow your weakness to incapacitate you.

You should activate your progress with the sowing of seeds. Your future lies in the seeds you sow today. Sowing seeds of progress into people's lives, especially the less-privileged, sets you up for your own progress. You can do this by counseling people, supporting them to start a business, providing training opportunities, etc.

It is also beneficial to sow seeds in the lives of people who have gone before you. Doing this brings their blessings into your life.

What you sow never leaves your life. You are always better off sowing (Proverbs 11:24-25).

Seek knowledge

You need knowledge to excel in life. Knowledge of God, world/general affairs, health, career, business, etc. You are a victim of your ignorance. The difference between a progressing believer and a stagnant one is knowledge. It is the dividing line. Daniel, in Daniel 9:2, said he understood by books. By giving himself to knowledge, he understood God's prophecy and the correct application of it.

Only those who have knowledge of their God will be strong and do exploits (Daniel 11:32). How will you gain knowledge of God if you do not dedicate yourself to studying His word?

Seek information, knowledge, and education. According to The Economist, the world's most valuable resource is no longer oil but data. Data, simply put, is information.

It is what you are informed about that forms your knowledge base. Knowledgeable people, all things being equal, make good leaders.

Don't be locked up in your world. Get out of your comfort zone and pick the brains of other people. Be hungry for information. Be an avid reader.

It is knowledge that will bring that much-desired ministry, career, business, and educational progress. It will give you an edge over your contemporaries because knowledge is power (2 Peter 1:3).

Be diligent

Diligence is careful and persistent work or effort. It is one thing to do something perfunctorily. It is another thing to do it well and right.

Aspire to run the race of life diligently and intentionally. Guide against distractions. They will hamper your productivity and cause you to lag behind. Run it to win the prize (1 Corinthians 9:24).

Set standards for yourself and determine not to go below them. Be a person of principles; be one of your words. An 'anything goes' mentality draws you back in the race of life. Guard yourself against laziness and slothfulness in everything that you do (Proverbs 22:29).

Ask for it

Desire progress and ask for it because, if anyone will receive it, it will be the askers (John 16:24; paraphrased). Progress is a product of God's mercy. The way of a man is not in himself, and no one can have anything on earth except it is given from heaven (John 3:27). The power of increase is with God.

Progress is His children's bread, and God is ready to give; therefore, ask **(Hosea 2:21-22).**

You must always acknowledge your need for God's assistance. Sometimes, you need a man's assistance. Ask God to tell you who to approach for help. It is God who gives power for progress; ask Him for it.

Be led by the Holy Spirit

Having the leading of the Holy Spirit guarantees sustained progress. He knows and teaches all things. The Holy Spirit is the pathfinder in the wilderness of life.

He knows the strengths and weaknesses of every individual, since He was present at creation. He knows how your weakness can be turned into strength. God has committed Himself to leading us through His Spirit, therefore, give Him a chance in your affairs (Psalm 32:8–9).

The Holy Spirit seeks to guide you in all your life endeavors – business, marriage, career, ministry, etc.

Juggling jobs does not guarantee success. The devil wants you to go your own way, so you can be frustrated. Move by the cloud of glory. because that is the secret of distinction. If a man misses his cloud, he signs in for a life of struggle and defeat. When you cede control of your life to the Holy Spirit, you enjoy His leading (Number 9:23).

Anytime you see that you are getting off course with God, return. Until you return to Him, it will not be your turn for outstanding progress.

Associate

Keep the company of people who are moving forward so that you can draw inspiration from them. No one has a monopoly on knowledge; therefore, don't be locked up. Relate with men of progress, so you will not get off the relay of success.

Do not fraternize with unprogressive people because they will poison your heart. Their presence in your life puts you on edge because your perspectives are not aligned. Motivational speaker Jim Rohn says that we are the average of the five people we spend the most time with.

You are either inspired or discouraged by the company that you keep. If you are not inspired, you will expire. Don't get expired, relate! (Proverbs 13:20).

In your relationships with people, you will see that you all make progress at different rates. Guard your heart against envy and wish everyone well. Be excited at the lifting of others.

Talk right

Engage in healthy conversation, and do not keep company with people who celebrate problems and failures. The words you speak today are the seeds for your harvest. Seed and harvest time shall not cease, for as long as the earth remains (Gen. 8:22). No matter what the economy or political situation around you, say what the God of Progress says.

If you share their confessions, you will also share their experiences. You will reap the rewards of what you sow, no doubt.

Be obedient

In the school of progress, obedience to God is not optional. It is a must for everyone who desires success.

Obey the leading of God in your heart and the instructions in the Bible. Often times, God's leading may look unappealing. However, since God is the originator of the instruction, greatness will ultimately be your identity (Isaiah 1:19).

Obey God in his charge not to defraud others. Progress in God answers to obedience to spiritual injunctions from the word of God.

Don't delay your workers' salary when it is due for payment. Wealth gained dishonestly will diminish. (Proverbs 14:31).

Live thankfully

To remain progressive, you must be a giver of thanks. You should be grateful to God for every increase you see in life. Nothing is too small to be thankful for. God is your source.

Don't allow the devil to deceive you into thinking otherwise. Gratitude opens the heavens over your life.

Jesus Christ gave thanks as he proceeded to feed the multitude. He gave thanks to God before handing the loaves over to his disciples for distribution to the multitude (John 6:5–12). You can increase the supply of food in your house with Thanksgiving. Lack of thanksgiving provokes the anger of God.

Over and above thanksgiving, determine to live thankfully. When we are grateful, we give thanks in all and despite all situations. Thanksgiving and living pave the way out of stagnancy. It guarantees abundance and preserves blessings.

Avoid wastage

God, even though he desires abundance for His children, is very opposed to waste. He expects you to seek out ways to utilize and save the resources He blesses you with.

Prodigal living will always bring nakedness and poverty. One of the ways to save our resources is to put them to good use. Any item we no longer need should be given out or sold. Keeping things we have no need of is a sign of selfishness. When we declutter our homes, we create room to receive more.

As a businessman, God expects you to intelligently and wisely transact your business. If you are a waster, the heavens over you will be shut. Let's see how Jesus approached this issue during His earthly journey.

After they fed the multitude, Jesus Christ asked his disciples to gather up the remaining food (John 6:12-13).

The fragrance you need at home can come from those fragments. The business capital you are looking for can come out of those unnecessary expenses. It will amaze you how much you can save by spending less. Your 'twelve baskets' are in the left overs. That unused car deteriorating in your garage could be the answer to somebody's problems. Has that ever occurred to you? Have you ever thought that selling it could help you offset some of your bills or loans? Your school fees can be paid because you chose to make the most of your time. You can engage in a business venture.

Every prodigal act puts you on the expressway to the camp of the swine. Don't lead yourself there!

Avoid giving excuses

Excuses, they say, are the nails used to build the house of failure. You are supposed to be an asset and not a liability in the kingdom of God. You are not a minus to this generation, but a plus. You are programmed to shine. You are destined to win after the order of Jesus (Luke 1:32).

Your progress will happen by design and not by accident. You will never be successful by chance. You will not be intentional about your life when all you do is give excuses for your inabilities.

The adventure of progress will not be easy. Intimidation will come in all shapes and sizes. Your determination to succeed will keep you from making excuses. All successful people have crossed hurdles and failed at some point.

You have to deal with all your excuses, or they will deal with your destiny. Excuses will keep you moving around in circles. This, of course, is not progress. Movement is not synonymous with progress.

You can fly high in your chosen field. You can be the go-to person in your organization. Do not allow negative circumstances to weary your soul. Toxic workplace practices - harassment, bullying, politics, etc., will attempt to drain your energy. Seek the face of God to know the best way to tackle these challenges. Do not use them as excuses to throw in the towel.

It is helpful to know that excuses are not self-existent. They are made by men. If that is the case, they can be unmade.

You will excel in your academics if you quit making excuses and do the needful. Academic success will answer to intentional studying. Your business will take a turn for the better if you pay attention to business acumen development ideas.

God will give you the vision. You will decide whether or not you will fulfill it.

In the school of life, like all schools, overtaking is allowed. If you join the queue, it may never get to your turn. Be determined, don't give excuses, and be the best version of yourself.

Take responsibility

Taking responsibility for your actions involves owning up to the positive and negative outcomes of your choices and behavior. It is a sign of maturity that causes us to be concerned about how we treat other people (Proverbs 28:13).

Your responsibilities to your family should motivate you to look out for them. Your sense of duty to the kingdom of God should propel you to be involved in community activities. Your love for God is evidenced by your commitment to people's progress. It is by so doing that the heavens will continually remain open over your life.

"Buck passing" is an act of irresponsibility. You should not shift blame or expect other people to carry out your duties for you. When you do this, your personal growth is hindered, and your progress is obstructed.

Taking responsibility for your actions matures you and guarantees your progress in life. Refusal to do so sets you up for a life of stagnation. Make your choice! God wants you to contribute to the progress of society. He wants you to be a blessing to humanity.

Like Elisha, turn the bitter water in your community to sweetness (2 Kings 2:19–22). Let the love of God be expressed through you.

Anytime you dodge your responsibilities, you truncate your blessings, because you will miss out on your seasons of growth. In your workplace, always be willing to go the extra mile. Consider this story about four people: everybody, somebody, anybody, and nobody. There was an important job to be done, and everybody was sure that somebody would do it. Anyone could have done it, but nobody did.

Somebody got angry about that because it was everybody's job. Everybody thought anybody could do it, but nobody realized that everybody wouldn't do it.

It ended up that everybody blamed somebody when nobody did what anybody could have done. This story sums up this section very aptly.

Trust God

Trusting God will deepen your relationship with Him. When you trust Him, you commit Him to your affairs. Trust Him for the perfection of your affairs and lean on His grace (Proverbs 3:5-6).

You cannot claim to have faith in God if you cannot trust Him. Conversely, you cannot trust God if you have no faith in Him.

The Holy Spirit enable us to make progress.

And I thank Christ Jesus our Lord, who hath enabled me, for that he counted me faithful, putting me into the ministry. 1 Timothy 1:12

The Holy Spirit is the divine enabler who empowers us to make progress in ways that go beyond our natural ability. When we walk in step with the Spirit, we tap into a supernatural source of strength, wisdom, and guidance that propels us forward on our journey. Progress made by the power of the Holy Spirit is not just human effort—it is divinely inspired movement, full of purpose, grace, and impact. The Spirit doesn't just help us move, He empowers us to move in alignment with God's will, unlocking doors, breaking barriers, and transforming us into who we are meant to be.

1. The Spirit as Our Guide

The Holy Spirit is not just a passive presence in our lives—He is our guide, leading us toward greater progress. When we yield to His direction, He illuminates our path and gives us the clarity we need to move forward with confidence. In moments of confusion or uncertainty, the Holy Spirit provides insight and understanding, showing us the next step to take. His guidance ensures that our progress is not random, but purposeful, always moving us closer to God's plan for our lives. "But when He, the Spirit of truth, comes, He will guide you into all truth" (John 16:13).

2. Empowered Beyond Human Ability

Progress made in our own strength can only take us so far, but when the Holy Spirit empowers us, we move beyond the limitations of human ability. The Spirit infuses us with divine energy that enables us to accomplish what we never could on our own. He gives us strength when we are weak, courage when we are afraid, and endurance when we feel like giving up. With the Holy Spirit, we move from striving to thriving, because His power is made perfect in our weakness (2 Corinthians 12:9). We don't just progress; we overcome, thrive, and excel because we are fueled by God's limitless strength.

3. Revelation and Wisdom for Progress

True progress requires more than just action—it requires revelation and wisdom. The Holy Spirit provides both. He reveals truths that we would not be able to see with our natural eyes and grants us wisdom to navigate complex situations. This divine revelation ensures that we make the right moves at the right time. Progress in partnership with the Holy Spirit is marked by divine timing—He opens the doors we are meant to walk through and closes the ones that would lead us astray. "For the Lord gives wisdom; from His mouth come knowledge and understanding" (Proverbs 2:6).

4. Transforming Us from the Inside Out

The Holy Spirit enables us to make progress not just externally, but internally. He works in us to transform our character, attitudes, and desires. As He molds us to be more like Christ, our internal growth reflects in every area of our lives. This inner transformation is the foundation for lasting progress. When we allow the Holy Spirit to work on our hearts, we experience breakthroughs in areas we've struggled with for years. He breaks chains, renews our minds, and makes us into new creations (2 Corinthians 5:17). The more we are transformed, the more progress we make, both spiritually and practically.

5. Grace to Persevere

One of the greatest gifts the Holy Spirit gives us is the grace to persevere. Progress is rarely smooth; there will be obstacles, delays, and challenges along the way. But the Holy Spirit strengthens us in times of difficulty, giving us the grace to keep going when we feel like giving up. He reminds us of God's promises and renews our hope, enabling us to press on in faith. With the Spirit, setbacks are not the end—they become stepping stones toward greater growth. The Holy Spirit equips us to endure, ensuring that our progress is steady and unstoppable (Romans 5:3-5).

6. Unlocking Spiritual Gifts for Progress

The Holy Spirit is the giver of spiritual gifts, and these gifts are key tools for making progress in both our personal lives and in advancing God's Kingdom. Whether it's the gift of wisdom, leadership, discernment, or prophecy, the Spirit equips us with specific abilities that empower us to serve and succeed in our calling. When we operate in our spiritual gifts, we make progress that glorifies God and fulfills our purpose. These gifts are not just for the benefit of others; they enable us to grow into the fullness of who God created us to be. "There are different kinds of gifts, but the same Spirit distributes them" (1 Corinthians 12:4).

7. Breaking Barriers and Strongholds

The Holy Spirit empowers us to break through barriers that would otherwise hold us back. In areas where we feel stuck or bound, the Spirit sets us free. He breaks strongholds—mental, emotional, spiritual, or even physical—that prevent us from progressing. Whether it's fear, doubt, unforgiveness, or sin, the Holy Spirit gives us the power to overcome anything that stands in the way of our progress. "Now the Lord is the Spirit, and where the Spirit of the Lord is, there is freedom" (2 Corinthians 3:17). This freedom enables us to move forward unencumbered, making progress that would have been impossible without His intervention.

8. Aligning Us with God's Will

One of the most profound ways the Holy Spirit enables us to make progress is by aligning our hearts and desires with God's will. Progress without purpose is meaningless, but when the Holy Spirit aligns us with the will of God, our progress becomes a fulfillment of divine destiny. He redirects us when we go off course, and He helps us discern God's direction for our lives. When we are in step with the Spirit, we make progress that is not just temporal, but eternal. "For it is God who works in you to will and to act in order to fulfill His good purpose" (Philippians 2:13).

9. The Spirit as Our Intercessor

The Holy Spirit also intercedes for us, praying on our behalf when we don't even know what to pray for. He advocates for our progress, ensuring that God's will is accomplished in our lives. In moments when we feel lost or overwhelmed, the Holy Spirit prays with groanings too deep for words (Romans 8:26). His intercession empowers us to make progress even when we don't have the strength or clarity to pray for it ourselves. With the Spirit as our intercessor, we are never alone on our journey—God is always working behind the scenes to help us move forward.

In summary, the Holy Spirit is the ultimate enabler of progress. He is our guide, strength, wisdom, and source of empowerment. When we walk in the Spirit, we move with a power far greater than our own, and the progress we make reflects both personal growth and the fulfillment of God's purpose in our lives. With the Holy Spirit, we break barriers, persevere through challenges, and achieve more than we ever could on our own. He leads us into deeper transformation, equips us with spiritual gifts, and aligns us with the will of God, ensuring that our progress is not just forward movement, but a divine journey of purpose, victory, and grace.

CHAPTER 12

WALKING WITH JESUS

Walking with Jesus gives us an assurance of His presence. It is impossible to be unaware of a person walking beside you. Constantly spending time in God's presence will distinguish you from other people. You carry His fragrance, aura, and imbibe His values. As you continue to keep company with Him, you begin to talk like Him. Without any doubt, He can send you on assignments to represent Him.

Furthermore, we are strengthened and are thus able to absorb the pressures of life. The peace that attends to us passes human understanding (Philippians 4:7).

God's Presence: Man's Qualifier

What qualifies a man for preferential treatment is God's presence in his life. Abraham, the father of faith, walked with God, and his testimony continues to speak (Genesis 17:1).

When you walk with Jesus, you carry His aura because you are constantly in His presence. Another thing that happens is that you become more like Him.

Enoch so walked with God that God took him. (Genesis 5:24). Fellowshipping with Jesus will make you a voice for Him because He will teach you His precepts and grant you utterance. David reaped the fruit of being in a good relationship with God. His enemies were delivered into his hands.

"¹The LORD said unto my Lord, Sit thou at my
right hand, until I make thine enemies thy
footstool.

Psalm 110:1

People who walk with Jesus are to be envied. They live by
the secrets of God; therefore, their influence is felt for
generations to come.

Regrettably, many Christians refuse to walk with God. They
work for Him, not with Him. God needs you to bond deeply
with him more than He needs you to work for him. He wants
you first! After all, if you refused to worship Him, He could
easily find a replacement for you (Amos 5:4-6).

Gilgal and Bethel were places of worship associated with
stones and the golden calf. God is saying that your attention
should be on Him and not on idols. When something is an
idol to you, it becomes more important to you than God.
Examples of idols are oneself, relationships, material
possessions, etc.

Walking with Jesus means we follow the leading of the Holy
Spirit all the days of our lives. This is living spiritually, and
everyone should embrace it.

I can see every wall of partition between you and God
breaking right now, in Jesus' precious name!

The secret of progress in God lies with Him. Remain
committed to your fellowship with him.

You will not benefit from your fellowship with God if you
are not meek. A meek person is able to bear heavy burdens

without complaining. Moses was the meekest man to ever live (Numbers 12:3). Moses learned a lot during his 40 years in the wilderness. God doesn't keep company with goats but with sheep. You can become the latter by yielding to His leading (Romans 6:13).

Benefits of Walking with Jesus

Walking with Jesus is not a religious activity or adherence to a set of rules. When we continually fellowship with the Holy Spirit, He breathes His life into us, and we experience unusual blessings. Here, we look at the compelling benefits of walking with Jesus, as contained in the word of God. These benefits serve as a testament to the richness and abundance found in a life surrendered to Christ.

Eternal salvation

At the heart of the Christian faith lies the promise of eternal salvation through Jesus Christ (John 3:16).

Through faith in Christ, we are reconciled to God and granted the gift of eternal life. This assurance frees us from the bondage of sin and empowers us to live with hope and confidence in the promises of God.

Forgiveness of sins

In Christ, we find forgiveness and redemption for our sins (Ephesians 1:7). Through His sacrificial death on the cross, Jesus atoned for our sins and made reconciliation with God possible. As we confess our sins and repent, we receive God's forgiveness and experience the liberating power of His grace.

Peace beyond understanding

The peace that Jesus offers surpasses all human understanding. Jesus Himself assures us of this in John 14:27. Peace is not dependent on external circumstances but is rooted in our relationship with Christ. As we abide in Him, we experience a deep and abiding peace that sustains us through life's trials and tribulations.

Abundant life

Jesus promises abundant life to all who follow Him wholeheartedly (John 10:10). This abundant life encompasses spiritual fulfillment, emotional wholeness, and purposeful living. Through our union with Christ, we discover the true meaning of existence and experience a richness of joy and satisfaction that cannot be found elsewhere.

Guidance and direction

Walking with Jesus provides us with guidance and direction for every aspect of our lives (Proverbs 3:5-6). As we surrender our will to God and seek His guidance through prayer and meditation on His Word, He faithfully directs our steps and leads us along the path of righteousness.

Strength in weakness

In our moments of weakness, Jesus offers strength and empowerment through the Holy Spirit (2 Corinthians 12:9 - 10). When we acknowledge our limitations and rely on God's strength, He equips us to persevere in faith and overcome obstacles.

Comfort in suffering

Walking with Jesus brings comfort and solace in times of suffering and adversity (2 Corinthians 1:3-4). As we entrust our cares to God and lean on His promises, He sustains us with His presence and surrounds us with His love.

Freedom from bondage

Through Jesus Christ, we are liberated from the bondage of sin and set free to live lives of righteousness and holiness (Galatians 5:1). As we yield to the transforming power of the Holy Spirit, we break free from the chains of sin and embrace the liberty found in Christ.

Intimate relationship with God

Walking with Jesus cultivates an intimate relationship with God, characterized by love, intimacy, and communion (John 15:5). Through prayer, worship, and fellowship with other believers, we deepen our connection with God and experience the fullness of His presence in our lives.

Assurance of God's love

In Jesus Christ, we find the ultimate expression of God's love for humanity (Romans 5:8). This sacrificial love serves as a constant reminder of God's faithfulness and commitment to His children. As we embrace the depth of God's love, we are transformed from the inside out and compelled to love others in the same manner.

Community and Fellowship

Walking with Jesus connects us to a community of believers who provide support, encouragement, and accountability

(Hebrews 10:24-25). As we share our faith journey with others, we are strengthened and experience the richness of Christian fellowship.

Hope for the future

In Jesus Christ, we find hope for the future and assurance of God's promises (Jeremiah 29:11). Despite the uncertainties of this world, we anchor our hope in the unchanging character of God and the certainty of His promises. Our hope is not based on wishful thinking but on the immutable word of God. It assures us of His faithfulness.

In conclusion, walking with Jesus is a transformative journey that offers profound benefits and blessings beyond measure. From eternal salvation and forgiveness of sins to peace, strength, and hope, the riches found in Christ are inexhaustible. As we embrace the abundant life that Jesus offers, we experience the fullness of God's love, grace, and provision. May we continually abide in Christ, drawing near to Him in faith and obedience, and may His presence permeate every aspect of our lives, guiding us along the path of righteousness and leading us to our eternal home.

CHAPTER 13

DEMONSTRATING YOUR KINGSHIP

The roles of kings and priests differ. As kings, we are expected to rule and reign, showing characteristics like compassion, loyalty, strength of character, humility, etc.

As priests, we should be prominent in religious systems and activities. We should stand as intercessors between God and His people and offer sacrifices and gifts on behalf of the people (Revelation 1:6).

Jesus Christ: The King of Kings

Jesus Christ is the king of kings. He is right now seated at the right hand of God in heaven, having vacated the earthly realm for us to rule and reign. He handed over power and authority to us.

> "[21]So Jesus said to them again, "peace to you!
> As the father has sent me, I also send you.
>
> John 20:21

Redemption confers greatness, honor, and dignity on you. All these are for public demonstration of the glory of God. Every king rules and reigns; therefore, we are to rule and reign in life (Romans 5:17).

To facilitate the actualization of your kingly and priestly roles, two instruments are made available to you.

Your Word

The parts of the coronation service are the recognition, the oath, the anointing, the investiture, which includes the crowning, the enthronement, and the homage. A royal staff, a symbol of regal authority, is handed over to newly enthroned kings. The coronation service is incomplete without the performance of this exercise. You are a king and your staff of authority is the word of God.

> "4Where the word of a king is there is power;
> and who may say to him, "what are you doing?
>
> Ecclesiastes 8:4

God did not have to frantically pace around to create the world. He sent His word, and everything aligned with it. In the same way, it will take you speaking to your world to dominate it. Just as God sent His word and the world obeyed, your world will obey your word.

You are God's voice. So speak, and the earth will respond. Your word is your messenger. Send it on an errand! The earth is commanded to hear the word of the Lord in Jeremiah 22 29.

God will back up your word if it is premised on His word. It was because Jezreel released His word that God sanctioned the release of his blessings. Natural kings do not struggle to get their counsel carried out. As a spiritual king, you need not struggle to establish your progress.

For your word to be law, the word of God must dwell in you richly. It is from this fullness that you speak, and things happen (Hebrew 4:12).

Angels

Angels, like God, are entirely spirits without material bodies. This quality makes them unchangeable and unlimited by any natural phenomenon. Humans do not have the same status; we consist of spirit and matter, so we change and die.

Angels exist for the sake of believers. They are sent by God to care for and protect them. Many Christians have never taken the pains to learn about them. Although God has placed humans a little lower than them, we are not supposed to worship them (Psalm 8:5). In heaven, we will be higher than them (I Corinthians 6:3).

> "[13]But to which of the angels has ever said: sit at my right hand, till I make your enemies my footstool? [14]Are they not all ministering spirits for those who will inherit salvation?
>
> Hebrews 1: 13-14

In the meantime, send your angels on errands. Usually, they work discreetly. They've been known to carry messages, fight battles, and even deliver food. Please deploy them anytime the need arises.

Co-Rulership with Christ

The roles of kings and priests are distinct, yet both are vital in fulfilling God's purpose in the world. As kings, we are called to rule and reign, taking dominion in various aspects of life while reflecting God's heart through our leadership. Kingship is not just about power or authority; it is about embodying compassion, loyalty, strength of character, and humility in a way that glorifies God and blesses others.

1. Ruling with Compassion
As kings, we are tasked with exercising compassionate leadership. True kingship isn't about ruling with an iron fist—it's about leading with a heart that cares for the well-being of others. Compassion moves us beyond self-interest and into service. We rule not to be served, but to serve. Just as Jesus, the ultimate King, showed compassion to the lost, the sick, and the broken, we are called to extend grace and mercy to those under our influence. Compassionate kings understand that leadership is stewardship, and the people we lead are God's treasures.

2. Loyalty to God's Will
A key characteristic of kingship is loyalty—first and foremost, loyalty to God and His will. As kings, we must be unwavering in our commitment to God's purpose for our lives and the territories we are called to oversee. Loyalty means standing firm in righteousness, even when the world pressures us to compromise. We are loyal to God's truth, His commands, and His calling, understanding that our authority as kings is derived from His authority. "Seek first the kingdom of God and His righteousness, and all these things will be added to you" (Matthew 6:33). When our loyalty is aligned with God, we rule with integrity and justice.

3. Strength of Character in Leadership
Being a king demands a strong moral and spiritual backbone. Strength of character is what separates those who lead for selfish gain from those who lead with God's heart. Character is the foundation of lasting leadership. As kings, we are called to make decisions that reflect honesty, integrity, and wisdom. The world often equates strength with dominance,

but in the Kingdom of God, true strength is found in righteousness, patience, and the ability to make sacrifices for the greater good. "The righteous are bold as a lion" (Proverbs 28:1). Strength of character enables us to lead boldly without being swayed by fear, greed, or ego.

4. Humility in Authority

Humility is one of the most vital characteristics of a godly king. True kings understand that their power and authority come from God, not from themselves. Humility reminds us that we are stewards of the authority given to us, not owners of it. Even as we reign, we must do so with a humble spirit, acknowledging that every victory and every success is the result of God's favor, not our own greatness. "Humble yourselves before the Lord, and He will lift you up" (James 4:10). Humility allows us to serve others without the need for recognition, making our leadership more impactful and authentic.

5. Taking Dominion with Wisdom

As kings, we are called to take dominion over the areas we are entrusted with—whether that's in business, family, community, or ministry. But this dominion must be exercised with wisdom and discernment. Godly kingship is about bringing order and peace to the domains we oversee, not chaos or division. Wisdom enables us to make sound decisions that lead to the flourishing of those under our care. Like King Solomon, who asked for wisdom to govern God's people, we must constantly seek divine wisdom to rule justly and effectively. "If any of you lacks wisdom, you should ask God, who gives generously to all without finding fault" (James 1:5).

6. Bringing Justice and Righteousness

One of the hallmarks of a king is the ability to administer justice and righteousness. As kings in God's Kingdom, we are called to defend the cause of the weak, protect the vulnerable, and ensure fairness in all our dealings. Our rulership should reflect the justice of God—upholding what is right and standing against what is wrong. Righteous kings do not turn a blind eye to injustice; instead, they confront it head-on, ensuring that the scales of justice are balanced. "He has told you, O man, what is good; and what does the Lord require of you but to do justice, to love kindness, and to walk humbly with your God?" (Micah 6:8). A king's strength lies in his commitment to God's justice, not worldly power.

7. Exercising Authority with Accountability

Kingship involves authority, but with that authority comes accountability. A true king understands that they are accountable not only to the people they lead but ultimately to God. We will one day give an account for how we have stewarded the authority and resources entrusted to us. Knowing this keeps us grounded, preventing us from abusing power or becoming corrupt. Accountability ensures that our reign is marked by responsibility and integrity, always keeping the will of God at the center of our leadership.

8. Building Legacy Through Service

As kings, we are called to build lasting legacies that honor God and benefit future generations. A king's legacy is not measured by how much power they amass, but by how much they serve and impact the lives of others. Jesus, the King of kings, left a legacy of servant leadership, washing His disciples' feet and sacrificing His life for the salvation of humanity. In the same way, our kingship should be defined by a heart of service, using our influence to elevate others and advance God's Kingdom. "The greatest among you shall be your servant" (Matthew 23:11). A legacy of service outlasts any throne or title.

9. Reflecting God's Heart for People

Finally, as kings, we must always reflect God's heart for His people. We are His ambassadors on earth, and how we lead should reflect His love, grace, and compassion. Every decision we make, every policy we enforce, and every action we take should mirror God's desire for His people to prosper, live in peace, and grow in faith. As kings, we are not just ruling over people; we are stewarding God's creation, ensuring that everything under our care flourishes according to His will. "For I know the plans I have for you, declares the Lord, plans to prosper you and not to harm you, plans to give you hope and a future" (Jeremiah 29:11).

In conclusion, the role of a king is one of responsibility, service, and divine authority. We are called to rule and reign, but to do so with a heart that reflects God's character—marked by compassion, loyalty, strength of character, humility, and justice. Kingship in God's Kingdom is not about dominance, but about stewardship—leading in a way that uplifts others and honors God. When we lead with these characteristics, we don't just rule—we transform lives, build lasting legacies, and advance the Kingdom of God on earth.

See you at the top!